LANDSCAPE MEANINGS AND VALUES

TITLES OF RELATED INTEREST

Agriculture: policies and people
P. Lowe *et al.* (eds)

Australian historical landscapes
D. N. Jeans (ed.)

City in the mind
P. Holt (ed.)

The countryside: planning and change
M. Blacksell & A. Gilg

Countryside conservation
B. Green

Development and the landowner
R. Goodchild & R. Munton

Discovering landscape in England and Wales
A. Goudie & R. Gardner

Edwin Lutyens
R. Gradidge

The imagined city
J. Arnold (ed.)

In a green shade★
R. Mabey

The life and work of John Nash, architect
J. Summerson

London's Green Belt
R. Munton

National Parks
A. & M. MacEwen

Nature's place
W. Adams

Nature's ideological landscape
K. Olwig

The open air museum
D. N. Jeans & P. Spearritt

Spoils and spoilers
G. Bolton

Valued environments
J. Burgess & J. Gold (eds)

William Talman
J. Harris

★ Not available from Allen & Unwin in North America.

LANDSCAPE MEANINGS AND VALUES

Edited by

EDMUND C. PENNING-ROWSELL

School of Geography and Planning
Middlesex Polytechnic

and

DAVID LOWENTHAL

Department of Geography
University College London

London
ALLEN AND UNWIN
Boston   Sydney

Allen & Unwin (Publishers) Ltd,
40 Museum Street, London WC1A 1LU, UK

Allen & Unwin (Publishers) Ltd,
Park Lane, Hemel Hempstead, Herts HP2 4TE, UK

Allen & Unwin, Inc.,
8 Winchester Place, Winchester, Mass. 01890, USA

Allen & Unwin (Australia) Ltd,
8 Napier Street, North Sydney, NSW 2060, Australia

First published in 1986

British Library Cataloguing in Publication Data

Landscape meanings and values.
1. Landscape   2. Nature (Aesthetics)
I. Penning-Rowsell, Edmund C.
II. Lowenthal, David
719'.01   QH75
ISBN 0–04–710003–6

Library of Congress Cataloging-in-Publication Data

Landscape meanings and values.
"Report of a symposium organised by the Landscape
Research Group and held on 4–6 April 1984 at the Royal
Institution, London, and Down Hall, Essex" – Pref.
Includes bibliographies and index.
1. Landscape assessment – Congresses.   2. Landscape
architecture – Congresses.   I. Penning-Rowsell, Edmund.
II. Lowenthal, David.   III. Landscape Research Group
(Great Britain)
GF90.L36   1986   712'.01   86–7980
ISBN 0–04–710003–6

Set in 10 on 11 point Bembo by Nene Phototypesetters Ltd, Northampton
and printed in Great Britain by Billing and Sons Ltd, London and Worcester

Foreword and acknowledgements

During the summer of 1983 the Landscape Research Group received a generous donation from a Foundation in the United States. There were no conditions attached to the gift, other than that it must be used for some purpose or purposes consistent with the aims and objectives of the Group as set out in its constitution.

The Board of Directors of Landscape Research Group Limited accepted the gift with gratitude and appointed a Committee under the chairmanship of David Lowenthal, Professor of Geography at University College, London, to recommend to the Board the most fruitful way of using the funds.

During the autumn of that year the Committee came to the conclusion that a meeting or meetings of some sort should be held in England during the spring of 1984 with a view to exploring the theme of 'Meanings and Values in Landscape', and recommended to the Board accordingly.

The Board duly authorised the same Committee to proceed with the making of detailed plans for the holding of a working party which would discuss a number of topics under that general title.

The view had been expressed by the Board that there were two desirable objectives. These were, first, that participation in the proceedings should be open to the Group's membership and indeed to the public on the widest practicable basis but, secondly, that the working party should be small enough to conduct its business efficiently and that this business should lead, if possible, to the production of a publication.

It was soon recognised that these two objectives could not be reconciled in one single event and consequently two meetings were arranged. The working party was to be held at Down Hall in Essex from the evening of 4 April to the afternoon of 6 April, 1984. Participation was to be by invitation and it was envisaged that those who accepted would find themselves, in a literal interpretation of the phrase, 'working'!

The fact that a proportion of the donated funds was to be used to cover the expenses of speakers from overseas who had been invited to take part in the working party added weight to the argument that the wider membership of the Landscape Research Group should be given the opportunity to benefit from their presence in England. It was recognised that if this larger meeting were to take place before rather than after the working party then it would enable the wider membership to make an effective if less exacting contribution to the eventual outcome of the venture, namely the present publication, by feeding in ideas which the working party could take up in its discussions.

Accordingly a one-day meeting was arranged to take place at the Royal Institution, London, on 4 April, and this was addressed by the six speakers who had been asked to prepare 'position papers' for prior circulation to the members of the working party. Each member had been asked to submit written comments on the papers, and on the basis of these comments a programme was devised for the meeting at Down Hall.

Following the two meetings the Landscape Research Group invited Edmund Penning-Rowsell and David Lowenthal to undertake the editorship of the present volume.

That, briefly, is how this volume came to be produced. The Landscape Research Group is deeply grateful to Professors Lowenthal and Penning-Rowsell, to the Committee to all the invited speakers, to the participants at the meetings in London and at Down Hall, to Lynda MacMillan who was responsible for all the practical arrangements, to the officers of the Landscape Research Group for carrying the additional work-load with a characteristic absence of complaint, and in particular to the American Foundation on whose generosity the whole undertaking has depended.

Jay Appleton
Chairman, The Landscape Research Group, 1984

Editors' preface

This volume comprises a report of a Symposium organised by the Landscape Research Group and held on 4–6 April, 1984 at the Royal Institution, London, and Down Hall, Essex.

Chapter 1 provides a summary of the background to and aspirations for this symposium, while Chapters 2 to 7 give papers prepared by landscape researchers eminent in their different fields and pre-circulated to the symposium's Down Hall participants for comment. At the end of each chapter we have made a brief selection of Critiques and Queries from these comments, chosen deliberately to highlight alternative views from those expressed in the author's contributions; the many commending comments are not included here.

Chapter 8 attempts to incorporate the many and diverse facets of the four workshop discussion sessions held at Down Hall. The essay is compiled in part from detailed notes by Carys Swanwick and Andrew Gilg, and was completed with comments from Hugh Prince, Ralph Cobham and Dick Watson. Inevitably some discussion points may have been omitted and, also inevitably, the essay may in parts seem self-contradictory owing to the attempt to represent diverse and often conflicting viewpoints.

Chapter 8 ends with a list of suggestions for further landscape research. This list has also been compiled from contributions from the Down Hall participants, with duplications omitted. We hope it will help to chart some future directions for landscape research and for the continuing activities of the Landscape Research Group.

Edmund C. Penning-Rowsell
Middlesex Polytechnic

David Lowenthal
University College London

Contents

List of tables

List of figures

List of plates

1 *Introduction*

DAVID LOWENTHAL

The study of landscape involves a paradox. Landscape is all-embracing – it includes virtually everything around us – and has manifest significance for everyone. Most scholarly disciplines and practical enterprises impinge on it in one way or another. Indeed, we all make our homes, do our work, and experience life in what we term landscape. It would be difficult to imagine a topic of greater importance than our relations with the world around us, in all its natural, altered, and man-made variety.

Yet virtually nothing is known about landscape as a totality. Landscape meanings and values vary from place to place and from epoch to epoch in ways that are little understood and seldom compared; we do not even know which landscape attachments are universal and which are specific to a particular time or place. How landscapes are identified and thought about; what components and attributes are discussed and admired; what symbolic meanings and physical properties they embody; how purpose, intensity, duration, realism, novelty, or impending loss affect our landscape experience – these are questions of immense import for which we have few if any answers.

Such lacunae in our understanding of landscape reflect not only the enormous scope of the subject matter it embraces but the paucity of landscape generalists. Most of us are concerned with only a tiny fraction of its multifarious meanings and uses: we are farmers or foresters or hikers or painters, seldom all these roles together. And very few of us make landscape our central concern.

Thus although landscape is a subject of generally acknowledged importance, integrated understanding of it is almost entirely lacking. The sheer multiplicity of interests that impinge on landscape – economic, aesthetic, residential, political – suggest the magnitude of the subject but at the same time seem to preclude the development of any unified perspective.

Over the past 15 years, the Landscape Research Group (LRG) has emerged as a group uniquely representative of almost the whole range of such interests. The LRG is perhaps the only organisation devoted to the study of landscape from every conceivable point of view. Two dozen LRG symposia held over the past 15 years cover a spectrum of academic and practical topics involving all the sciences and arts, and embracing most types of environments and landscape uses.

These explorations have been exciting and beneficial, enlarging the horizons of all concerned. We felt it would now be desirable to order these interests and realms of expertise within a more coherent framework that might help us to explore the whole range of landscape concepts and uses in an interrelated fashion. To this end, the LRG convened a symposium of Meanings and Values in Landscape in England in the spring of 1984. The generosity of a benefactor enabled us to cast our net beyond our usual parameters and enlist the participation of eminent individuals both in Britain and America to produce working papers on their different ways of shaping, viewing and using landscapes. The general aims of the symposium, and of this volume, were as follows.

(a) To review concepts about landscape that are explicit or implicit in the arts, the sciences, and among landscape practitioners and users, and to organise these concepts to see how they resemble, differ from and interrelate with one another.

(b) To survey the range of interests and uses to which landscapes are put and examine their collaborative or conflicting nature.

(c) To assess and categorise the values, past, present and future, ascribed to landscape.

(d) To review the range and impact of specific actions which affect the character and use of landscape.

(e) To pinpoint lacunae in landscape understanding where research is especially needed, to provide leads for future landscape-related research that might promote the process of synthesis, and to explore how such syntheses might be extended on an international scale.

No definitive conclusions were expected; instead we sought to point the way toward future work which might revise current perspectives. The conference and this volume summarising its results are not meant to be a summing up but a starting point, not a conclusion but the beginning of a new exploration.

2 An ecological and evolutionary approach to landscape aesthetics

GORDON H. ORIANS

A central problem in the study of human biology is to determine the extent to which our current behaviour patterns have been moulded by our long-term evolutionary history. Identifying which human behavioural characteristics are highly modifiable as a result of experience, and which are more resistant to changes because they are more constrained by genetically-based properties of the nervous system, is an extremely difficult task. There are severe limits on the ways people can be studied, and investigators are influenced by the high level of emotions generated by implications that might be labelled 'biological determinism'. Indeed, it is currently impossible to engage in rational discourse on many aspects of the evolution of human behaviour because a majority of people, including scientists, hold such powerful *a priori* opinions about them.

In this complex but important arena, the study of human responses to landscapes and plant shapes offers unusual possibilities. Because selection of places in which to live is a universal animal activity, there is a considerable body of theory and data upon which to build hypotheses specifically oriented toward human behaviour (Charnov 1976, Levins 1968, MacArthur & Pianka 1966, Orians 1980, Partridge 1978, Rosenzweig 1974, 1981). In addition, because choice of habitat exerts a powerful influence on survival and reproductive success, the behavioural mechanisms involved have been under strong selection for millennia.

In all organisms, habitat selection presumably involves emotional responses to key features of the environment. It is these features that induce the 'positive' and 'negative' feelings that lead to settling or rejection. If the strength of these responses is a key proximate factor in decisions about where to settle, then the ability of a habitat to evoke such emotional states should evolve to be positively associated with the expected survival and reproductive success of an organism in that habitat. Good habitats, as measured by the features that contribute to survival and reproductive success, should evoke strong positive responses while poorer habitats should evoke weaker or negative responses. Basic responses to habitat features are likely to be modified by the presence of other individuals of the same species, both because they provide information about choices made by previous arrivals and because those individuals modify the quality of the environment (Orians 1980). Also, responses depend on the stage in the life-cycle of an organism, that is what particular resources are of greatest value to it at the moment.

For species other than *Homo sapiens*, these emotional states are currently unknown to us. We can observe only changes in individuals in response to alterations in the intrinsic quality of available habitats and densities of individuals in them. Human emotional responses, however, are directly accessible through verbal communication and the written word. In addition, the great capacity of people to change environments provides a source of information not available for the studies of other species that effect relatively minor alterations to their surroundings.

In this chapter I first present an overview of current thinking about habitat selection and, secondly, explore the implications of this body of knowledge for human responses to landscapes and plant shapes. Thirdly, I suggest ways of testing these ideas and review the tests that have already been made. Finally, I relate these ideas to more general notions about the evolution of a sense of beauty among people.

Habitat selection theory

Organisms choose places in which to perform activities for a variety of reasons and their decisions affect the locations of their activities for varying lengths of time. It is convenient to view the process of selecting sites in a hierarchical framework (Charnov & Orians 1973). The number of levels identified is arbitrary, but it is useful to recognise four of them, corresponding to choice of (a) habitat, (b) patch, (c) behavioural mode, and (d) responses to specific objects (Fig. 2.1).

In this scheme, a *habitat* is considered to be a collection of environmental patches large enough such that the organism in question can carry out a significant part of its life cycle within that

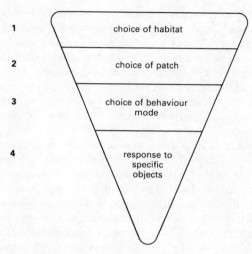

Figure 2.1 A hierarchical model of habitat selection (after Charnov & Orians 1973).

piece of terrain. For a migratory bird, a habitat would be an area in which it could complete breeding activity during the summer or, in the tropics, an area large enough to meet its survival needs for the winter. For an insect living inside a leaf and finding sufficient food inside that leaf to grow from the egg to the pupal state, the single leaf constitutes its habitat.

A *patch* is a piece of terrain that is internally homogeneous and different from other types of patches in the habitat. Since no two places are absolutely identical, the notion of homogeneity is a relative one. Decisions about which units to recognise as patches must be made on the basis of knowledge about the organism being studied and how it uses the environment.

Within a patch, an organism may carry out any of a large number of activities, such as feeding, defending space, courting, bodily maintenance, hiding, sleeping and nesting. Usually a single activity dominates the attention of an individual at any moment in time because most of these activities are mutually exclusive. Each activity requires a *behavioural mode*, such as hunting, advertising or building, and the mode may change abruptly as when the arrival of a predator terminates courtship. The end result of the adoption of a behavioural mode is the encounter of objects, animate or inanimate, that are potentially suitable as prey, mates, rivals, or sleeping places. At that point an individual must decide whether or not the object is sufficiently high in quality that it merits being eaten, courted, threatened or slept in. Selection of habitat determines the quality and quantity of patches and objects likely to be encountered by the organism during the course of its activities, sometimes for the duration of its life. Consequently, habitat selection mechanisms have been under the strong influence of natural selection in most species.

Imagine an organism searching through an environment looking for a habitat in which to settle. It constantly encounters new sites which it evaluates as either being worth further exploration or not. Which decision it makes depends both on the intrinsic quality of the site in relation to the best of all possible sites, how many sites of varying quality the animal has already found and rejected, and how much time remains for continued searching. The first type of information is the basis on which the individual can judge the overall quality of sites in the general area in which it is searching. The poorer the set of habitats already encountered, the more likely an animal is to accept a less than optimal site (Levins 1968). Similarly, the higher the risk of searching, the lower the threshold of acceptance (Fig. 2.2). Thus, animals of most species are unlikely to possess simple mechan-

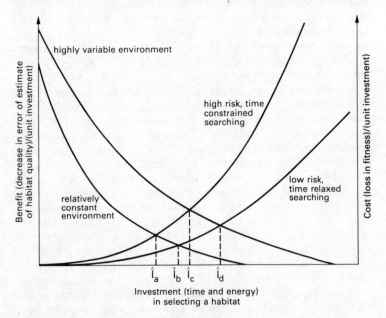

Figure 2.2 A cost–benefit model of habitat selection (from Orians 1980).

isms of acceptance and rejection of habitats. Rather they are likely to have *responses* conditional on such things as past experience, time constraints, and physiological condition.

Actual selection of a site involves several important stages. The first is the decision whether or not to explore the site further. If this decision is positive, the second stage is one during which the organism gathers information. The third stage is the actual decision to remain for the set of activities appropriate for that time of year or part of life-cycle. The information used in these three stages is not likely to be the same. Exploration of a strange environment may be dangerous because the individual lacks information on the presence or absence of predators, whether they are most likely to be hiding, and the location of the best escape routes. Therefore, the first reactions of an animal are likely to be a mixture of positive responses that may induce exploration and fear of the consequences of exploring unfamiliar terrain. During the exploration stage, as the animal becomes more familiar with the site and more comfortable in being in it, attention is increasingly directed toward assessing the availability of resources, but fear probably never disappears because life is dangerous even in familiar environments and predators may appear suddenly in unexpected places.

Because a suitable habitat must provide resources for carrying out many different activities over substantial time periods, evaluation of habitats is a difficult process. The current state of the environment is important, but probable future states over the entire time span during which the site will be occupied may be equally, if not more, important to survival and breeding success. Many temperate zone birds, for example, choose breeding areas in spring before the food supplies that will support breeding are present and before the flush of vegetative growth appears that will profoundly alter the habitat. Clues used in selecting habitats should be good predictors of future states if they are to serve as effective guides for settling behaviour.

For this reason, the proximate clues to which organisms respond may not be the same factors as the ones that ultimately determine success. For example, birds appear to use general patterns of tree density and branching arrangements to determine where to settle (Hildén 1965, Lack 1971) rather than attempting to assess food supplies directly. The structure of vegetation is likely to be a reasonably good predictor of the types of food items that will be present one or two months later, as well as of the ways in which a foraging individual must manoeuvre in the environment to find and capture those foods. For other organisms, however, proximate and ultimate clues may be the same. Female parasitic insects identify hosts on which to lay their eggs and can even determine if another parasite has already laid on or in the host. Because the latter is key to the probabilities of their offspring surviving, many of the conditions that the developing larva will encounter over its life can be assessed directly.

Human life-cycles, in contrast, are very long. A single breeding cycle from conception to independence of offspring lasts about two decades, but habitats are not necessarily occupied for that length of time. In fact, over much of our evolutionary history people have been strongly nomadic, occupying many sites during the course of a single year in response to seasonal changes in resource availability (Geist 1978). Therefore, the time spans relevant to many habitat choices made by people are short in relation to total human life-span.

The evolution of curiosity

Exploration of habitats is costly in terms of time and energy and potentially exposes the explorer to higher risk of predation than if it remained in the protection of familiar cover. Long-term contributions to survival and reproductive success provide the explanation for performing such explorations, but the immediate motivator appears to be curiosity (Berlyne 1960). Organisms are highly motivated to explore and will work hard even when the reward is simply an opportunity to view an environment (Harlow et al. 1950). An important research objective is to identify the patterns of environmental configurations that induce exploratory behaviour and to relate those to intrinsic features of environments that contribute to fitness.

Both familiar and unfamiliar environments are capable of generating strong involvements (Kaplan & Kaplan 1982), there being an evident trade-off between the excitement of new environments and the comfort generated by familiarity. How these two components interact is poorly understood and considerable research is needed to determine how patterns of response change as familiarity is increased through exploration and residence.

The complexity of an environment is another important component of its ability to arouse feelings (Kaplan & Kaplan 1982). Very simple environments are immediately comprehended so that further exploration is unlikely to yield additional information which is useful in making an assessment. Furthermore, given the complex needs of human existence, simple environments may lack essential life-support elements. At the other extreme, very complex environments may repel an observer because an initial viewing of the scene reveals no patterns that could be better comprehended with further exploration. Landscapes at intermediate levels of complexity evoke the strongest desires to explore. An observer in a laboratory responding to an unfamiliar scene projected on a screen is probably emotionally in the first stage of the habitat selection process. The response being measured is: 'would I like to explore this environment further?'

The theme of the importance of safety in initial responses to landscape scenes has been developed in some detail by Appleton (1975) in his book *The experience of landscape*. His conception is built on the notion that the risks of exploration can be reduced if the environment offers sites where good visibility (prospect) is possible but where the observer is at the same time hidden (refuge). Thus, the observer is afforded an opportunity to gain information about the environment while at the same time preventing other organisms from obtaining information about the viewer. Appleton argues, with many examples, that highly motivating scenes provide both prospect and refuge, although interesting landscapes obviously include a considerable range in the ratios of these two components. One possibility is that scenes with a higher prospect : refuge ratio become more motivating as the familiarity of the observer with them increases, and hence risks associated with being in the environment decrease, but to date no analysis has been made of this possibility.

Approaches to the study of human landscape preferences

It is reasonable to view human responses to landscapes as an example of habitat selection mechanisms. As such, they should reflect the powerful natural selection that has undoubtedly acted on those response patterns. Evidence of those patterns can be obtained by a variety of means, each of which provides insights not available through the others. I direct my attention here to three of these: the structure of landscapes manipulated primarily for aesthetic reasons; responses to photographs of landscapes; and how environments are portrayed in paintings.

Aesthetic environments

People in all cultures manipulate vegetation for aesthetic purposes, although the degree to which that art has been developed is strongly and positively correlated with cultural stability and affluence. Major investments in aesthetic manipulations appear only when basic survival needs are fully satisfied, concerns with pleasure loom large in peoples' senses of satisfaction with life, and there is high expectation of being able to enjoy these places long enough to make it pay to alter them.

Many habitats are modified primarily for utilitarian purposes, such as food production, transportation or sports. They may have aesthetic value, but their basic design is determined by other considerations. However, parks and gardens are generally designed purely for the pleasure they give. Therefore, these environments should reflect evolutionarily based preferences better than should utilitarian environments. Indeed, the greater aesthetic appeal of manipulated environments compared to 'natural' ones has been eloquently expounded by Dubos (1976).

Although parks and gardens are created primarily for aesthetic purposes, they are also influenced by other considerations. For example, modifying large expanses of land requires large sums of money. Development of large parks and gardens also requires social tranquility and relative freedom from fear of attack by enemies. The structure of gardens may change as the level of security increases (Carpenter *et al.* 1974). Differences in species of plants available to work with, in societal ideals and symbols, and in attitudes towards nature also influence the forms of gardens and parks (Tuan 1974). However, if evolved habitat preferences exert a significant influence on the structure of aesthetic habitats, then some common features should underlie the many variations characteristic of intra- and inter-cultural differences in garden styles.

A large body of evidence shows that much of human evolution took place in the savannas of East Africa (Geist 1978, Leakey 1963, Robinson 1963), even though the most recent stage has been played out in the Mediterranean region. The savannas of tropical Africa have high resource-providing potential for a large terrestrial, omnivorous primate. In tropical forests, most primary productivity occurs in the canopy, and a terrestrial omnivore largely functions as a scavenger, gathering up bits of food that fall from the more productive canopy. In savannas, however, trees are scattered and much of the productivity is found within two metres of the ground where it is directly accessible to people and to grazing and browsing mammals. Biomass and production of meat is much higher in savannas than in forests (Bourliere 1963, Bourliere & Hadley 1970, Dasmann 1964, Hopkins 1967, Lamprey 1964, Sinclair & Norton-Griffiths 1979, Wiegert & Evans 1967).

Drinking water, needed by people and grazing animals alike, is less available in savanna environments than in wetter forest regions, and movements of large mammals are strongly influenced by availability of dry-season water (Sinclair & Norton-Griffiths 1979). Fortunately, game abundance and dry season water co-vary in East Africa – their abundance fluctuates together over space – and most early human fossil sites are likewise associated with riparian and lacustrine locations (Boaz 1979a,b, Behrensmeyer 1975, 1978). In still drier areas, both production of meat and available water further decrease. Therefore, savanna environments should have been of higher quality for early human existence than either wetter or drier habitats (Orians 1980).

If these surmises are generally correct, and if we assume that habitat preferences co-evolve with intrinsic quality of habitats, then certain predictions follow. First, savanna-type environments with scattered trees and copses in a matrix of grassland should be highly preferred environments for people and should evoke strong positive emotions. This prediction is borne out in the broad sense in that environments manipulated strictly or primarily for the pleasure they evoke are generally savanna types (Orians 1980). Parks and gardens in all cultures are neither closed forests nor open grasslands. In addition, great pains are taken in the creation of parks and gardens to create water or the illusion of water, or to enhance the quality and quantity of existing water resources.

The second prediction is that the tree shapes characteristic of highly productive habitats should be preferred over those shapes characteristic of either drier or moister habitats in the tropics. This general prediction leads to two more specific ones that are amenable to direct testing. The first is that given the array of species from which early gardeners could select those to use in their manipulated environments, those with natural shapes more similar to the savanna models should have been preferred over those species with shapes more divergent from the savanna models. Second, subsequent modifications of those trees, whether by genetic selection or pruning, should be such as to make them more like the savanna models than the wild grown forms.

These two predictions have been the basis of some preliminary tests. We have determined those ecological features correlated with high availability of game, water and safe sleeping places in Kenya and then measured the shapes of dominant trees in those habitats as well as in drier, less productive savanna and scrub habitats and in moister riparian habitats. Trees in the habitats

Table 2.1 Characteristics of Kenyan savanna trees and large shrubs (means ±1 standard deviation).

Group	Species	Number of branches at trunk	Total height vs. mean canopy width	Trunk height vs. total height
high quality savannas	*Acacia drepanolobium*	2.07 ± 1.72	0.89 ± 0.24	0.36 ± 0.24
	Acacia etbaica	2.20 ± 0.63	0.97 ± 0.14	0.20 ± 0.10
	Acacia hockii	2.10 ± 0.32	0.63 ± 0.15	0.16 ± 0.14
	Acacia nilotica	2.24 ± 0.56	0.66 ± 0.24	0.15 ± 0.11
	Acacia senegal	1.90 ± 0.32	0.97 ± 0.28	0.51 ± 0.13
	Acacia seyal	2.36 ± 0.92	0.71 ± 0.17	0.12 ± 0.09
	Acaia tortilis	3.00 ± 1.00	0.71 ± 0.17	0.27 ± 0.11
	Delonyx elata	3.00 ± 0.67	0.93 ± 0.13	0.11 ± 0.04
	Adansonia digitata	4.30 ± 1.34	1.04 ± 0.26	0.34 ± 0.09
	Sterculia sp.	4.10 ± 1.66	0.85 ± 0.18	0.12 ± 0.06
riparian	*Acacia elatior*	3.40 ± 1.08	1.08 ± 0.13	0.10 ± 0.04
	Acacia xanthophloea	3.00 ± 1.05	1.16 ± 0.44	0.14 ± 0.07
	Ficus sycomorpha	3.80 ± 1.62	1.22 ± 0.29	0.10 ± 0.05
	Tamarindus indica	3.40 ± 1.08	1.33 ± 0.39	0.10 ± 0.06
	Trichilia roka	4.10 ± 1.29	1.57 ± 0.37	0.12 ± 0.09
drier savannas	*Acacia mellifera*	2.60 ± 0.70	0.76 ± 0.12	0.10 ± 0.08
	Balanites sp.	2.73 ± 0.79	0.99 ± 0.23	0.10 ± 0.14
	Boschia sp.	5.50 ± 2.80	1.03 ± 0.32	0.14 ± 0.18
	Commiphora africana	2.60 ± 0.97	0.84 ± 0.19	0.24 ± 0.12
	Commiphora campestris	2.60 ± 0.70	0.75 ± 0.04	0.20 ± 0.07
	Commiphora madagascarensis	2.10 ± 0.57	0.86 ± 0.19	0.29 ± 0.11
	Commiphora rivae	2.70 ± 0.95	0.71 ± 0.12	0.22 ± 0.10
	Tarchonanthus camphoratus	7.70 ± 3.27	0.97 ± 0.28	

judged to be ecologically optimal are broader than they are tall, have canopies wider than they are deep, have small, compound leaves, and have trunks that are short relative to the total height of the trees (Table 2.1). Riparian trees are taller relative to their width and have trunks that are somewhat taller relative to the total height of the tree than do the savanna species. In drier habitats the savanna trends are accentuated: many of the species lack trunks altogether and absolute heights are greatly reduced (Plate 2.1).

Wild grown trees of species chosen for use in gardens, and those not chosen, were also studied, this time in Japan (Table 2.2). Among maples (*Acer*), one of the dominant genera of trees in Japanese gardens, chosen species differ from non-chosen species in being broader relative to their height, in having relatively shorter trunks, and in having smaller, more deeply divided leaves. Garden and wild grown individuals of chosen species do not differ in shape because garden maples are not pruned but allowed to assume their normal growth patterns (Plate 2.2). Chosen oaks (*Quercus*) do not differ from non-chosen oaks in any general growth form features, but all chosen species are evergreen and have relatively small leaves whereas none of the deciduous species, all of which are large-leaved, are planted as ornamentals in formal Japanese gardens.

None of the conifers commonly used in Japanese gardens grow naturally with forms resembling those of African savanna trees, but the Japanese red pine (*Pinus densiflora*) does change its form in windswept locations, such as seashores and mountain ridges. This clear evidence of malleability may have attracted early Japanese gardeners. Unlike maples, garden conifers in Japan are highly modified by pruning, being induced to grow broader than tall, with trunks that branch close to the ground and with foliage trimmed to produce a distinct layering similar to that characteristic of a number of African savanna trees.

Our limited Japanese data suggest that growth form similar to that of savanna trees was one of the criteria that may have been subconsciously employed by early Japanese gardeners in selecting

Table 2.2 Intrageneric comparisons of chosen vs non-chosen Japanese plants (★ = significantly different at $P = 0.05$); summary data on Kenyan trees are shown for comparison.

Group	Species	N	Total height vs. mean canopy width	Trunk height vs. total height	Canopy depth vs. canopy width
chosen	*Acer*	18	1.25★	0.27	0.94
non-chosen	*Acer*	48	1.52★	0.31	1.02
chosen	*Quercus*	15	1.56	0.27	1.09
non-chosen	*Quercus*	30	1.66	0.27	1.17
Kenya	optimal	—	0.83★	0.24★	0.64★
Kenya	riparian	—	1.25★	0.11★	1.12★
Kenya	dry	—	0.85	0.19★	0.68

Table 2.3 Intraspecific comparisons of shapes of wild and garden trees (★ = significantly different at $P = 0.05$).

Species	N	Number of branches at trunk	Number of main branches	Total height vs. mean canopy width	Trunk height vs. total height	Trunk height vs. trunk circumfer-ence	Canopy depth vs. canopy width
Acer palmatum (wild)	10	2.80	6.20	1.12	0.21	3.66	0.87
Acer palmatum (garden)	23	2.48	6.13	1.15	0.25	3.21	0.89
Quercus glauca (wild)	6	2.67★	6.83	1.34	0.23	3.57	0.99
Quercus glauca (garden)	10	5.40★	7.80	1.44	0.37	5.48	0.88
Pinus densiflora (wild)	9	2.70★	3.10★	2.15★	0.76★	11.74★	0.47
Pinus densiflora (garden)	42	5.67★	9.98★	0.98★	0.56★	1.98★	0.55
Podocarpus macrophyllus (wild)	1	2.00	2.00	2.00	0.65	12.26	0.70
Podocarpus macrophyllus (garden)	11	5.27	8.18	1.68	0.39	5.09	0.91

broad-leaved trees for garden use, and that subsequent pruning, in species manipulated in this manner, has increased the similarity of those trees to the presumed savanna models. None the less, the data also indicate that many other factors have been at work in influencing choice of species in Japanese gardens.

Japanese gardens, being based primarily on tree and shrub shapes and not on flowers, are those most likely to demonstrate the patterns suggested by a tropical savanna-based model of landscape preferences. Other garden traditions, especially the formal gardens of western Europe, are clearly based on alternative aesthetic criteria. Most of them contain no individually conspicuous trees that are allowed to assume growth forms anything like natural ones, let alone savanna tree forms (Plate 2.3). In these cases geometric designs, and the importance of demonstrating the ability of the estate owner to dominate nature, override alternative criteria for design. Indeed, most of the formal gardens are not designed to be viewed by a person walking through them but rather from a higher vantage point, usually an upper storey of the home of the owner, further emphasising the role of the garden as a form of dominance display.

Responses to photographs of landscapes

When studying plants and animals we cannot ask organisms why they made the choices they did but can only infer choice criteria on the basis of observable behaviour. With humans we can take advantage of complex verbal communication to devise tests not possible with other species. The results are problematic because people may, for a variety of reasons, give unreliable accounts of their behaviour. They may not be aware of the true bases of their choices, may invent reasons to avoid embarrassment or to please the investigator, or they may have reasons to deceive. None the less, when used with care, these approaches offer powerful supplements to the observational method that formed the basis of our field work on plant form.

One of the best developed techniques for assessing people's preferences for landscapes is to present them with photographs of landscapes in which features such as tree shapes and densities, presence or absence of water, topography and signs of human habitation are controlled and varied to yield combinations of traits selected by the investigators (Kaplan *et al.* 1972, Kaplan 1977, Daniel & Boster 1976, Zube *et al.* 1974).

An interesting study using coloured slides matched for overall quality was carried out by Balling and Falk (1982). They showed that 8- and 11-year-old residents of the northeastern United States preferred scenes of tropical savannas to those of more familiar deciduous and conifer vegetation, but that from the age of 15 years until retirement age familiar scenes were equally preferred to those of tropical savannas. Tropical rain forests and deserts were given lower ratings by all age groups. Ratings of landscapes by persons who had less contact with rural scenes were, on average, lower than those of other people, but the qualitative relationships among the scenes are none the less the same.

The same techniques of presentation can be adapted to test people's preferences for particular tree shapes. We are currently engaged in such studies in co-operation with a psychologist, Dr J. Heerwagen. Our experimental design includes holding species of tree constant while varying its shape as much as possible, and holding species of tree constant while varying the density of trees in savanna scenes. Such studies can also reveal the importance of such features as the greenness of herbaceous vegetation on preference ratings of landscape scenes.

Landscape painting

Art is not merely a substitute for photography. Through distortions of reality, artists evoke emotional responses to their subject matter in the minds of viewers. Landscape painters strive to create scenes that either attract or repel (or both), depending on what is being portrayed (heaven, hell, wilderness, etc.). We have not as yet conducted empirical studies related to paintings and savanna landscapes. Furthermore the only detailed habitat-related analysis of landscape painting (Appleton 1975) does not address the savanna hypothesis directly, although any scene offering a good combination of prospect and refuge is likely to be a savanna. Closed forests are deficient in prospect while desert and grassland scenes are deficient in refuge.

Hypothesising further, it is instructive to ask whether landscape scenes are also crafted to capture emotions appropriate to the second stage of habitat selection, namely investigation. A good scene both induces a desire to explore further and, by the arrangement of its elements, channels the directions of the imagined exploration. Paintings, to be effective, should not only command the initial attention of the observer, but also have features that make people wish to view them many times. This is accomplished in part by designing a painting so that when the observer imagines himself or herself moving into the scene its content and the information to be obtained can never be resolved.

A winding path or road, or a meandering river, serve that function admirably because the observer can repeatedly postulate conditions 'around the bend' but can never determine what they are.

The roots of beauty

Human beings, like all other species, select habitats from an array of options and, like other species, display strong emotional responses to landscape configurations and plant shapes. An evolutionary perspective suggests that strong emotions generated by objects or situations signal the action of long-term natural selection for those responses. That habitats have functioned in this manner is not surprising. What is less obvious, however, is why the sense of beauty associated with certain landscape features is so strong.

The notion that the human sense of beauty might be amenable to biological analysis is not a new one. Indeed, in 1785, 70 years before Darwin published *On the origin of species*, the Scottish philosopher Thomas Reid suggested how a biologist might proceed:

> By a careful examination of the objects which Nature hath given this amiable quality (of beauty), we may perhaps discover some real excellence in the object, or at least some valuable purpose that is served by the effect it produces upon us. This instinctive sense of beauty, in different species of animals, may differ as much as the external sense of taste, and in each species be adapted to its manner of life.

In this remarkable passage Reid recognises that the aesthetic senses of animals are likely to be related to their ecologies and that the evolution of animal responses should be related to the functional significance of objects. Human beings, however, display a great diversity of reactions to landscapes and plants (and to many other objects, for that matter), a diversity so great that the only obvious conclusion is that there are no generalisable response patterns to be detected. Indeed, the diversity of human responses has led most observers to agree with Clive Bell that 'Any system of aesthetics which pretends to be based on some objective truth is so palpably ridiculous as not to be worth discussing' (Bell 1913).

If there is any truth in the perspective advanced by Thomas Reid and hinted at by me in the preceding pages, it must lie in the possibility that some common principles actually do underlie the apparent chaotic diversity. Indeed, Darwin's principle of natural selection postulates a general mechanism believed to be applicable to the evolution of the diverse properties of the millions of species of living organisms inhabiting the Earth. The theory of gravitational attraction occupies a similar position. One can, in fact, imagine the argument, fostered by the obvious fact that different types of objects fall at different rates and that some objects actually rise, that 'any theory that pretends to be based on a simple objective truth concerning the rates at which bodies fall is so palpably ridiculous as not to be worth discussing'.

With Newton's apple and Darwin's natural selection as stimuli to look for commonalities amongst diversity, we can explore briefly the possible evolutionary roots of beauty, mindful of the richness of human aesthetic responses.

As a starting point consider the behavioural consequences of having a sense of beauty. The most obvious one is that a thing regarded as beautiful attracts repeated attention: we keep looking at it. Associated with this attention is some sense of value: this object is better in some way than other objects regarded as less beautiful. Indeed, the father of scientific aesthetics, Santayana (1896), regarded the sense of beauty as a precursor to, or at least an indispensable part of, our concept of value. Thus, the sensation of beauty is triggered physiologically as mild arousal from perceiving some stimulus object that fits a conceptual pattern (Geist 1978). It is difficult to imagine feelings of beauty aroused by objects that we cannot 'understand'. The response that regards a tree or flower as beautiful depends on the prior existence of some concept of a tree or flower. It is difficult to appreciate new styles in music or art in part because the patterns do not make sense to us. Not until our tastes have been educated enough to recognise those new patterns is it possible for us to perceive some beauty in them.

Geist (1978) has persuasively argued that the aesthetic experience of beauty has one of its roots in a more functional evaluation of the value of objects for carrying out certain tasks. A beautiful axe to a person familiar with axes is a highly functional one. Similar responses are evoked by other functional objects. The concept of landscape beauty could well have similar roots because 'beautiful' landscapes are probably highly functional ones in that they potentially provide rich combinations of resources for human existence.

A second root of aesthetic preferences may stem from the importance of being able to classify objects and to place specific things in their 'proper' places. Classification is one of the great human passions. Intelligent people squander great fortunes in collecting and classifying objects. A stamp collector spends much time arranging stamps in an album, usually by country and, within country, by date of issue, taking great pride in the collection and making persistent attempts to complete particular series of stamps to 'fill out the page'.

To a non–stamp collector (or to a non–collector of any particular class of objects) it is obvious that stamp collecting is an activity without any apparent biological function. It is engaged in simply because of the pleasure it brings to its practitioners. This passion for collecting has not received much attention from psychologists even though Pavlov (1928) pointed out its importance many years ago.

It is equally clear that the pleasure of collecting resides not primarily in the accumulation of objects but in their assembly into some system which establishes and clarifies their inter-relationships. Recognising the patterns and the reasons for their existence is a prime source of the pleasure associated with collecting and classifying. It is also at the root of the appreciation of music and art. Haydn's Surprise Symphony is a surprise only to those who know the normal pattern of progression of notes in Baroque music. A novice detects nothing of interest. The ability of some of Prokofiev's music to evoke mirth also depends on recognition of the expected pattern so that the deviation from that pattern causes surprise and laughter.

Psychologists have long described human responses to pattern variation as *stimulus discrepancy*. People often respond with pleasurable emotions to minor variations in a familiar stimulus pattern but with negative feelings toward major deviations from the same pattern. Children's humour is characterised by responses to what are, to adult tastes, gross deviations from familiar patterns. The ultimate humour is, of course, telling a story in which the deviation from the pattern is so subtle that nobody else recognises it. The great social power of humour and laughing together is that it tells us that we have common knowledge and values and can recognise deviations from them. That one's associates laugh at the same jokes tells one a great deal about them and the extent to which they share one's values. The most difficult thing to understand in a foreign language is humour.

This view of the roots of beauty is capable of providing explanations for both the great diversity of aesthetic responses to some classes of things and the narrower range of responses to others. In music and art great variability is possible, and is eagerly sought because a large number of patterns can be created and learned and, once a new pattern is learned, variations on it can be recognised and appreciated. We do not know to what extent the kinds of musical patterns that can be appreciated by trained ears are limited by the basic structure of our nervous systems; such questions have not been asked and explored. None the less it is clear that the range of patterns capable of evoking senses of beauty is large.

With respect to landscapes, the range may be smaller because it is not just the ability to recognise patterns in landscapes that is pertinent. Rather, if the arguments advanced here have merit, only those environments emotionally associated with high re-source levels for people should be able to evoke strong positive responses. Exploration of this issue will require extensive testing among persons of different age, gender, and social status in a variety of cultures, but the small body of data now being gathered at least suggests that the range is limited. If so, the implications for urban design, landscaping, social aggression, therapy, and art, are powerful. At the very least, extensive exploration of these limits is worth the careful examination of objects that Thomas Reid suggested to us nearly 200 years ago.

Acknowledgements

Ideas presented in this chapter have been developed in part through conversations with Lionel Tiger, David Western, Judith Heerwagen, Jay Appleton and Elizabeth Orians. For helpful reviews of the manuscript I am indebted to Judith Heerwagen, Robert Benton and Elizabeth Orians. Our fieldwork in Kenya and Japan was supported by a grant from the Harry Frank Guggenheim Foundation.

References

Appleton, J. 1975. *The experience of landscape*. London: Wiley.

Balling, J. D. and J. H. Falk 1982. Development of visual preference for natural environments. *Environment and Behavior* 14, 5–28.

Behrensmeyer, A. K. 1975. The taphonomy and paleoecology of Plio-Pliocene vertebrate assemblages east of Lake Rudolph, Kenya. *Bulletin of the Museum of Comparative Zoology* 146, 473–578.

Behrensmeyer, A. K. 1978. The habitat of Plio-Pleistocene hominids in East Africa: Taphonomic and microstratigraphic evidence. In *Early hominids in Africa*, C. J. Jolly (ed.), pp. 165–89. London: Duckworth.

Bell, C. 1913. *Art*. London: Chatto and Windus.

Berlyne, D. E. 1960. *Conflict, arousal, and curiosity*. New York: McGraw-Hill.

Boaz, N. T. 1979a. Hominid evolution in Eastern Africa during the Pleistocene and early Pleistocene. *Annual Review of Anthropology* **8**, 71–85.

Boaz, N. T. 1979b. Early hominid population densities: new estimates. *Science* **206**, 592–5.

Bourliere, F. 1963. Observations on the ecology of some African mammals. In *African Ecology and Human Evolution*, F. C. Howell and F. Bourliere (eds). Chicago: Aldine.

Bourliere, F. and M. Hadley. 1970. The ecology of tropical savannahs. *Annual Reviews of Ecology & Systematics* **1**, 125–52.

Carpenter, P. L., T. D. Walker and F. O. Lanphear 1975. *Plants in the landscape*. San Francisco: W. H. Freeman.

Charnov, E. L. 1976. Optimal foraging: the marginal value theorem. *Theoretical Population Biology* **9**, 129–36.

Charnov, E. L. and G. H. Orians 1973. *Optimal foraging: some theoretical considerations*. Utah: University of Utah, Department of Biology.

Daniel, T. C. and R. S. Boster. 1976. *Measuring landscape esthetics: The scenic beauty estimation method*. USDA Forest Service Research Paper RM-107. Fort Collins, Co: Rocky Mountain Forest and Range Exp. Station.

Dasmann, R. F. 1964. *African game ranching*. Oxford: Pergamon.

Dubos, R. 1976. Symbiosis between the earth and humankind. *Science* **193**, 459–62.

Geist, V. 1978. *Life strategies, human evolution, environmental design: toward a biological theory of health*. New York: Springer-Verlag.

Harlow, H. G., M. K. Harlow and D. R. Meyer 1950. Learning motivated by a manipulation drive. *Journal of Experimental Psychology* **40**, 228–34.

Hildén, O. 1965. Habitat selection in birds. *Annals, Zoologica Fennica* **2**, 53–75.

Hopkins, B. 1967. A comparison between productivity in forest and savannah in Africa. *J. Ecol.* **55**, 19–20.

Kaplan, R. 1977. Preference and everyday nature: Methods and application. In *Psychological perspective on environment and behavior: theory, research and application*, D. Stokois (ed.). New York: Plenum.

Kaplan, S., R. Kaplan and J. S. Wendt 1972. Rated preference and complexity of natural and urban visual material. *Perception and Psychophysics* **12**, 354–6.

Kaplan, S. and R. Kaplan 1982. *Cognition and environment*. New York: Praeger.

Lack, D. 1971. *Ecological isolation in birds*. Oxford: Blackwell.

Lamprey, H. F. 1964. Estimation of the large mammal densities, biomass, and energy exchange in the Tarangire Game Reserve and the Masai Steppe in Tanganyika. *East Africa Wildlife Journal* **2**, 1–46.

Leakey, L. S. B. 1963. Very early East African Hominidae, and their ecological setting. In *African ecology and human evolution*, F. C. Howell and F. Bourliere (eds). Chicago: Aldine.

Levins, R. 1968. *Evolution in changing environments.* Princeton, NJ: Princeton University Press.

MacArthur, R. H. and E. R. Pianka 1966. On the optimal use of a patchy environment. *American Naturalist* **100**, 603–9.

Orians, G. H. 1980. Habitat selection: general theory and applications to human behavior. In *Evolution of human social behavior*, J. Lockard (ed.), pp. 49–66. New York: Elsevier.

Partridge, L. 1978. Habitat selection. In *Behavioural ecology: an evolutionary approach*, J. R. Krebs and N. B. Davies, (eds), pp. 351–76. Sunderland, Mass: Sinauer Associates.

Pavlov, I. P. 1928. 'The reflex of purpose', republished 1963, in *Lectures on conditioned reflexes*, Vol. 1. London: Lawrence & Wishart.

Robinson, J. I. 1963. Adaptive radiation in the Australopithecines and the origin of man. In *African ecology and human evolution*, F. C. Howell and F. Bourliere (eds). Chicago: Aldine.

Rosenzweig, M. L. 1974. On the evolution of habitat selection. In *Proc. First Internat. Congress Ecology*, pp. 401–4, Wagenigen.

Rosenzweig, M. L. 1981. A theory of habitat selection. *Ecology* **62**, 327–35.

Santayana, G. 1896. *A sense of beauty.* New York: Random House (reprinted 1955).

Sinclair, A. R. E. and M. Norton-Griffiths 1979. *Serengeti: dynamics of an ecosystem.* Chicago: University of Chicago Press.

Tuan, Y-F. 1974. *Topophilia: a study of environmental perception, attitudes and values.* Englewood Cliffs, NJ: Prentice-Hall.

Ulrich, R. S. 1977. Visual landscape preference: a model and application. *Man–Environ. Systems* **7**, 279–93.

Wiegert, R. G. and F. C. Evans 1967. Investigations of secondary productivity in grasslands. In: *Secondary Productivity of Terrestrial Ecosystems*, K. Petrusevicz (ed.), Vol. 2. Warsaw and Krakow: Institute of Ecology, Polish Academy of Sciences.

Zube, E. H., D. G. Pitt and T. W. Anderson 1974. *Perception and measurement of scenic resources in the southern Connecticut River Valley.* Amherst, Mass: University of Massachusetts Institute for Man and His Environment.

Critiques and queries

The criticisms listed here reproduce principally the *adverse* comments on the chapter, to show the divergence of views even amongst those intimately involved with landscape matters.

Ian Brotherton I liked this paper very much largely because Gordon Orians uses his discipline to generate relevant hypotheses *and* to pursue, or suggest, their testing. However he does present a number of debatable assertions (p. 11) on how environments manufactured for pleasure are essentially savanna, or how beautiful landscapes are highly functional. My main concern is how do we know when to 'buy' an evolutionary rather than a cultural explanation? Can we rely on Orians's assertion (p. 3) that strong emotions are produced by long-term selection? All commentators in this field appear to accept the views of everyone else: how do they differ from one another? They cannot all be right all the time, can they?

Denis Cosgrove   Frankly, I have very little sympathy with this paper. I do not doubt that as part of nature we intuit strong links between its processes and forms and those of our own bodies, and structuralist theory has suggested something of the consistency in the transformation rules that bring these into language and other social and cultural conventions. But such intuitions are so transformed, overlain and mediated by social, cultural and economic as well as personal meanings historically, that to trace the bio-physiological bases of environmental (*not* landscape) response seems largely futile at best, and at worst pandering to the most dangerously ideological interpretation of 'human nature'. The paper abounds in unfounded and unscientific assumptions.

John Gittins   Gordon Orians says (p. 20) 'only those environments emotionally associated with high resource levels for people should be able to evoke strong positive responses'. In part this may be true but I would remind readers of the following words of Gwyn Jones in *A Prospect of Wales*:

> But our words are numbered like the years, and the count is running out. So little is said, so much is left unspoken. For most of us, after all, the meaning of Wales, the knowledge that what we see and feel is not elsewhere offered over the whole world's surface, will be found not in the famed vistas, the showplaces, the triadic Wonders of the Island of Britain, but in some corner of a field, a pool under a rock, in a bare sheep-walk or a cottage folded in a gulley, in a hard road trodden by the feet of our fathers and their fathers before them; some private place that can never engage a general admiration, and for that is all the more dear.

> > Dim on lleuad borffor,
> > Ar fin y mynydd llwm;
> > A swn hen afon Prysor
> > Yn canu yn y cwm . . .

So sang a young Welsh poet killed in war. 'Only the purple moon at the edge of the bare mountain, and the sound of the old river Prysor singing in the valley.' How poignant and how immeasurable that 'only'. The moon, the mountain, and the river.

For these are radiance, grandeur, and song. All these are Wales, and these the best of Wales.

Muriel Laverack Gordon Orians's paper links 'habitat selection' with 'human response to landscape' too closely for me to accept. Valid perhaps when the ancestors lived in or beneath the trees, less so now when so many other factors shape 'habitat selection'. One emerged from the absorbing savanna hypothesis questioning the analysis's relevance now in landscape work. It may be provable to the satisfaction even of scientists that preference for certain tree shapes is a direct link with East African savanna origins of *Homo sapiens*, but what use is this to our understanding of the development, utility, quality of present landscapes . . . ?

Dick Watson I find the emphasis on coherence (p. 18) and high-resource levels (p. 20) somewhat limiting: there are periods in which the human response to landscape has preferred the fierce, wild, and the inhospitable. The challenge of mountain landscape is one example (see the romantics, especially Wordsworth, Byron, Shelley); the modern travellers in the deserts and rain forests are impelled by something which we might call the anti-coherent impulse. To be sure, these are unusual people; but they often set the tone and mood for others.

Gordon Orians replies: There are times in the development of any discipline when careful experimentation and testing of ideas are the prime needs. At other times, speculation to stimulate thinking about problems in different ways and to lead to new conceptualisations of issues are top priorities. My perspective as an evolutionary biologist is that the study of landscape aesthetics is in need of new concepts to give direction to future research. Only time will tell whether my own attempts to provide some of them will prove useful.

Meanwhile, it is important to recognise that the particular line of reasoning I have taken is only one of many that might be explored from an evolutionary perspective. I chose habitat selection as a reasonable starting point because, of all aspects of behavioural ecology, it seemed most relevant to environmental aesthetics. Even if habitat selection models are able to capture a significant component of the roots of landscape aesthetics it is already abundantly clear that they cannot capture all or even most of them. For example, models of territorial behaviour and social dominance are likely to prove more useful in understanding formal European gardens than are habitat selection models. Much may also be learned from studies of sensory physiology. The way patterns are perceived may have an important influence on the motivating power of designs, whether they be in fabrics, gardens, or natural vegetation. Another promising field is developmental psychology, viewed from an evolutionary perspective in which developmental patterns are seen as products of natural selection just as are other phenotypic traits.

The thrust of these comments is that the field of landscape aesthetics is likely to develop most rapidly if a wide variety of ideas is developed, explored, and tested. We already know that the problem is complex, but this is no reason to avoid taking bold conceptual steps. Inevitably our first attempts to develop new ideas will be incomplete. My critics have identified some weaknesses in my arguments but to expect the themes to be fully developed already is to ask for more than I or anybody else could deliver.

3 The role of the Arts in landscape research

JAY APPLETON

The Landscape Research Group has always been at pains to avoid defining with any precision what it means either by 'landscape' or 'research'. The Group has been content to allow an interpretation to emerge from the activities of its members, and the only qualifications expected of them are that they acknowledge an interest in landscape and pay their subscriptions. This may not seem a very scientific way of approaching 'landscape research'; nevertheless many members of the Group certainly see themselves as scientists and expect scientific standards to be maintained in the activities organised by the Group and in the material published by its organ, *Landscape Research*.

Most periodicals, I suppose, like most disciplines, can be seen as falling into one of two categories which we loosely call 'The Arts' and 'The Sciences'. We tend to think of them as employing different kinds of methodology, each of which is acceptable to, and indeed demanded by, its own practitioners. The prospect of the working methods, the philosophical assumptions, the conventions and the techniques, appropriate to the one, penetrating the jealously guarded domain of the other is likely to arouse in scholars sitting on either side of the fence a certain degree of anxiety for the integrity of their work. A researcher in the arts may feel threatened by the very idea of pouring the cold light of scientific enquiry on the delicate substance of the arts; but it is equally probable that the scientist will be profoundly concerned about the damage which may be sustained by a piece of scientific research, if it is allowed to become contaminated by unscientific methodology or emotion. Indeed the danger may be greater than that if as a result of one or two pieces of work being discredited the reputation of a whole organisation is put in jeopardy.

Consider this little poem:

BECK

Not the beck only,
Not just the water –
The stones flow also,
Slow
As continental drift,
As the growth of coral,
As the climb
Of a stalagmite.
Motionless to the eye,
Wide cataracts of rock
Pour off the fellside,
Throw up a spume
Of gravel and scree
To eddy and sink
In the blink of a lifetime.
The water abrades,
Erodes; dissolves
Limestones and chlorides;
Organizes its haulage –
Every drop loaded
With a millionth of a milligramme of fell.
The falling water
Hangs steady as stone;
But the solid rock
Is a whirlpool of commotion,
As the fluid strata
Crest the curl of time,
And top-heavy boulders
Tip over headlong,
An inch in a thousand years.
A Niagara of chock-stones,
Bucketing from the crags,
Spouts down the gullies.
Slate and sandstone
Flake and deliquesce,
And in a grey
Alluvial sweat
Ingleborough and Helvellyn
Waste daily away.
The pith of the pikes
Oozes to the marshes,
Slides along the sykes,
Trickles through ditch and dub,
Enters the endless
Chain of water,
The pull of earth's centre –
An irresistible momentum,

> Never to be reversed,
> Never to be halted,
> Till the tallest fell
> Runs level with the lowland,
> And scree lies flat as shingle,
> And every valley is exalted,
> Every mountain and hill
> Flows slow.

Norman Nicholson, 1981

How do we react to the idea of incorporating this kind of material into an investigative process which we expect to be regarded as a serious, scientifically acceptable enquiry?

The easiest reaction is to throw it out. It may be fun, all right in its place, but not here. If we allow what purports to be logical argument to be contaminated by what contains palpable un-truths, are we not putting at risk that part of our investigation – our 'message' even – which is based on scientifically acceptable methodology, and ought we not therefore to be very careful about admitting such 'alien' material?

It is my submission that a great deal of what the arts have to say about landscape is liable to present us with this sort of problem in some degree; yet it is in this very kind of material that we may find new insights which the rational, logical language of science cannot evoke. In any case, since the Landscape Research Group is constitutionally committed to the encouragement of inter-disciplinary co-operation it can scarcely solve the problem by excluding the arts or, for that matter, the sciences. At the very least they must be encouraged to co-exist as providers of parallel, if methodologically separate, approaches to landscape research. A more enterprising view, however, would envisage promoting an *integrated* methodology in which each contributes something distinctive towards the achievement of a common objective. Must we regard the arts and the sciences like oil and water, decreed by their very nature not to mix, or can we find something analogous to an emulsion in which their mutually repellant properties are overcome?

The prospect of a fruitful partnership between the arts and the sciences raises a number of important questions, all of which will be found to impinge closely on 'meanings' and 'values'. Since I think the accepted norms of scientific method are likely to be the less controversial element in the mixture, I propose to review briefly some of those problem-posing issues which are chiefly to be found within the arts, whether visual, graphic, literary, or of any other kind.

By approaching the problem in this way we may pose three questions:

(a) What progress have we made, and
(b) what progress may we reasonably expect to make towards achieving
     (i)   the co-existence, and
     (ii) the integration of the two methodologies in our investigations into landscape?

Scientific method/methodologies in sciences and the Arts

Before examining more closely the main methodological problems posed by the intrusion of the arts into the sciences, let us note one or two points about the scientific method itself. This is certainly not an essay on the philosophy of science, and we shall not dig deep, but even the most superficial examination will suffice to warn us of the dangers of falling into erroneous assumptions, such as that all scientific propositions, to be validated, must be subject to testing by replicable scientific experiments.

A chemist or a physicist who claims that the behaviour of physical matter is subject to the operation of general laws, which have been demonstrated by laboratory experiments, must indeed be prepared to accept that a repetition of those experiments which does not achieve the predicted results may be interpreted as a refutation of his hypothesis. These underlying assumptions are so much part-and-parcel of the methodology of the so-called 'pure sciences' that we may be in danger of overlooking the fact that many scientific investigations are not, and cannot be, of this kind.

Let us look at an example. A mineralogist, confronted by an unfamiliar mineral, may examine its optical properties and propose the hypothesis that it always displays the same characteristics when studied in thin-section under polarised light. The successful replication of experiments to test this hypothesis may result in its being accepted as a diagnostic tool by a geologist who, having discovered such a mineral *in situ*, may subject it to testing as many times as he thinks necessary. But if this same geologist believes that the occurrence of this mineral suggests that it was formed under particular geological conditions and formally proposes an hypothesis to this effect, he *cannot* call for an action-replay of the Caledonian Orogeny to establish whether his hypothesis is correct. A great deal of stratigraphical interpretation is based on hypotheses which are *not* capable of demonstration by replicated experiments, yet we do not say for this reason that mineralogists are scientists but stratigraphers are not.

Already, therefore, in considering the permissibility of admitting 'arts' techniques into their own domain, scientists must face the fact that susceptibility to testing by replicated experiments, culminating in predicted results, is not even a *shibboleth* which distinguishes the sciences and certainly is not a qualification which they have a right to demand of the intruder.

This said, let us look more closely at some of those attributes of the arts which may be a cause of unease among the more scientifically sensitive of our colleagues. It may help to clarify the issue if we recognise that within those arts which are concerned with landscape there are two levels of investigation which commonly may be identified.

(a) The investigation and interpretation of the environment by the artist (for instance in landscape painting or poetic description).
(b) The investigation and interpretation of works of art, objectives of art, theories of art, etc., by art historians, critics and other arbiters of taste.

The methodology of the latter has at least certain affinities with the methodology of the scientist, in that it involves the possibility of questioning, if not of outright refutation, by properly marshalled evidence. The process by which an hypothesis in this field may be challenged is broadly of the same kind as that by which one scientist might challenge the hypothesis of another. There is a general acceptance that the rules of logic apply. Among both art critics and scientists a fallacy is inadmissible; a *non sequitur* may be disastrous.

The methodology of the first type of investigation listed above, however, is not necessarily subject to the same constraints. We may indeed find logic, reason and method in a work of art but we cannot demand it. Merely to speak of a *non sequitur* in, say, a late Turner landscape would seem to most of us as strange; we might well question whether the phrase could have any meaning at all in such a context except, perhaps, in a strongly metaphorical sense.

To identify and describe an inconsistency in a landscape painting may help us to a more penetratingly rational appraisal of its meaning but not necessarily of its value. The most highly

valued paintings of the late Middle Ages and the Renaissance are
loaded with anachronisms and topographical absurdities. Hun-
dreds of Nativities are depicted in contemporary medieval
buildings which could not possibly have been constructed in the
reign of Herod, and set in landscapes which could never have
cradled the little town of Bethlehem. Yet few of us would regard
such criticisms of a painting as having any real relevance to its
value as a vehicle for expressing its message. We recognise that
the artist is using a channel of communication which gives him or
her the option of bypassing reason if they choose to go that way,
or to incorporate rational passages within a context which is
rationally inconsistent.

Land form, process and imagination

Let us look a little more closely at Norman Nicholson's poem,
which I have chosen to quote in full because he has clearly gone
out of his way to express in the language of poetry ideas which
have been advanced by scientists: geomorphologists, geologists,
geophysicists, hydrologists and others who have studied and
scientifically described the processes of denudation by which
uplands are reduced to peneplains.

There is little in Nicholson's words which deny what we might
call a 'consensus view' from the scientists about these processes.
There is, in fact, only one parameter in the whole phenomenon
which has clearly been distorted – grossly distorted – and that is
the time factor. It is this distortion itself which is the point of the
poem. When water falls over a cataract it moves at a pace which
allows us to form a visual image of a process of movement and not
just of a static shape. When we look up at the hills we see what
appear to be static shapes, because the processes of which they are
the interim products are of such immensely long duration that we
cannot form visual images of them *as processes*. 'Process' implies
movement, and what Nicholson does is to speed up this process
by employing the metaphor of rushing water so that shape and
process are brought into focus.

As a means of scientific explanation this may seem to be a
dubious device, because it clearly has recourse to making
statements which are not true in any literal sense. Yet it is but a
short step from a device commonly accepted in the documentary
motion-picture, where the film is, so to speak, 'speeded up'.
Shoots of plants can be seen emerging from the ground, buds
opening into blooms, clouds forming and dissolving with such

rapidity that the air movements causing their formation and dissolution can be comprehended by the observer as they occur. We do not say that this is unscientific, because we understand perfectly well that sequences of events have been converted from one time-scale to another.

Nicholson in fact tells us nothing which the scientists had not told us already. What he does is to restate ideas previously expounded in scientific prose, which appeals to our reason, in a new language. He does not exclude an appeal to reason. We are still expected to make a rational assent to those scientific interpretations on which he draws so heavily. But he drives, as it were, *through* reason to a different objective, the stimulation of the imagination.

It is my contention that the major role of the Landscape Research Group is to develop ways in which students of landscape can broaden their investigative effort to embrace every kind of source from which they may derive information useful for their purposes. Landscape architects, when discussing the technicalities of their own profession, would probably choose to do so within their own fraternity: the Landscape Institute, the American Society of Landscape Architects, or some such body. Similarly, art historians, literary scholars, conservationists, planners, horticulturists, etc., each have their own specialist organisations. But increasingly the more perceptive practitioners in all these fields are recognising that even the most technical argument needs a context, a wider framework to provide a proper perspective. The interdisciplinary approach to which members of our Group are committed qualifies it, I believe, particularly, perhaps even uniquely, to provide a forum in which we can all seek an understanding of the values and meanings without which our own more specialised interests are unlikely to make sense.

Problems and potentiality of 'evidence' or 'clues'

As researchers in a multidisciplinary field we must be sure that we know how to handle the subject matter of the arts and the sciences congruously, exploiting the potentialities of each without prejudicing the validity of the other. As an example of the kind of problem which is likely to lead to misunderstanding, controversy, even confusion, consider the ways in which we regard 'evidence' – evidence to support, to refute, to challenge or to modify the hypotheses by which we seek to explain the perceived environment. But evidence may be of many different kinds, lending itself to different uses and suffering from different limitations, and if we are to compare the arts and the sciences as potential sources of evidence, it is important to recognise this. One dictionary definition of evidence is 'support for a belief', and this concept raises all sorts of questions about the nature, degree and effectiveness of that support and about the stage in an argument at which it may be properly and usefully employed.

Although scientists will always, on reflection, admit that the word 'evidence' is susceptible of many kinds of interpretation, they generally think of it first and foremost as information which may be used to establish the validity of a hypothesis. If possible, to establish it in such a way and to such a degree of certainty that it will eliminate alternative possibilities and leave the hypothesis unimpaired. Other interpretations envisage 'evidence' in terms of the partial achievement of this end and, in so far as it falls short of fulfilling the ultimate criterion, it is to that extent inferior. On a *prima facie* interpretation it must often seem that the sort of evidence adduced by the arts tends to be of this kind, at best circumstantial, but that does not necessarily mean that it is unacceptable or unconvincing.

Consider this forensic analogy. A prosecutor in court, when marshalling his case, will have before him all the information he has been able to gather in support of his argument that the accused is indeed guilty of the crime which he is alleged to have committed. His business is to convince the court that the hypothesis he is advancing is supported beyond reasonable doubt by the evidence he puts forward. As far as possible he will choose to base his case on evidence which can neither be factually refuted nor interpreted in some alternative way which does not imply the involvement or the guilt of the accused. If, by including circumstantial evidence, he succeeds only in persuading the court that his case rests on that rather than on 'conclusive proof', he might do better to leave it out.

I think it is fair to say that most scientists would accept this forensic analogy as expressing something like the situation in which they find themselves when writing up the results of their researches, or reading a paper to a learned society. Once they have brought their argument to a stage where it can be presented with the authority which stems from thorough experimental testing, then inconclusive pointers – straws in the wind – are better left out, just as are those circumstantial snippets of information which a prosecutor is reluctant to present to the court.

What needs to be remembered, however, is that at an earlier stage in the investigation those same snippets of information may have been of crucial importance to the detective responsible for unravelling the story and furnishing the basis for the prosecution. He probably does not call them 'evidence' but 'clues'. Without them, and the importance he has attached to them, the case might never have come to court.

I believe that some of the unease which scientists may feel at the prospect of sharing an investigative process with their arts colleagues, involving, as it may well do, the use of a methodology which seems to them to lack the rigours of what they regard as respectable scientific practice, may be allayed if they see their respective contributions in this light. Nowhere is the truth of this more apparent than in research into landscape, where the available evidence is of such a wide-ranging kind.

Four 'areas of investigation' and problems

In very general terms the arts and the sciences may be commonly found to have distinctive roles to play in landscape research. As long as we understand that we are referring to loosely defined conceptual categories and not hard-and-fast divisions, I suggest three kinds of 'areas of investigation' based on the nature of the evidence used.

(a) Those principally reliant on 'scientific' evidence. For instance, the explanation of the distribution of natural vegetation may call for correlations between environmental conditions, such as soil types, acidity, the behaviour of groundwater, rainfall regimes, macro- and micro-climatic factors, and so on, on the one hand, and the occurrence and distribution of tree species on the other.

(b) Those in which 'mixed evidence' drawn from the arts and the sciences is involved, as, for instance, in the reconstruction of past landscapes when we are able to draw on evidence not only from surviving paintings, topographies and other literary records, but also from highly exacting scientific techniques such as pollen analysis and radio-carbon dating.

(c) Those in which evidence from the arts is dominant. This category may be further subdivided as follows:

(i) Areas in which the arts have a monopoly or near-monopoly of surviving evidence. As an example we could take the investigation of past landscape taste and the changes it underwent from one period to another as described in the pioneering paper by Lowenthal and Prince (1965). Their sources are very largely drawn from contemporary literature. The methods commonly used in present-day landscape evaluation, involving the testing of the reactions of respondents to landscape photographs, obviously cannot be applied retrospectively. We may be able to draw on the work of modern environmental psychologists to help us in our *interpretation* of the attitudes and preferences of former societies. But to discover what those attitudes and preferences were, we must rely principally on the evidence of the arts, because that is all that has survived.

(ii) Areas in which the arts have a different investigatory function from that of the sciences. There is a parallel here with the difference between evidence and clues, already alluded to, and this difference is particularly important in the early, speculative stage of our thinking. Of course, the arts have no monopoly of imaginative speculation. Without imagination, no inventive scientist could identify the most advantageous paths along which to press forward. But poets and painters are much more free to explore the *terra incognita* which lies beyond the advancing fronts of science. Already we have learnt a great deal about the human experience of landscape from their interpretations of what they have observed. However unscientific these interpretations may be, and any rejection of this source of enlightenment, simply on the grounds that the methods of the artist do not measure up to the standards demanded by science, would be as irrational as a military commander's refusal to heed the reports of his intelligence officers on enemy-held terrain simply because they had not yet actually visited the places and conditions they describe.

This concept of complementary but distinctive roles for the arts and the sciences invites us to think very hard about the opportunities and the limitations inherent in each. Consider, for instance, the question of particularity of time and space. A scientist might reasonably expect precision in both these dimensions and therefore become impatient with source material which appears to communicate information only vaguely and without clearly defined limits of application. To date a landscape as a work of art is one thing; to date its content, its subject, and its 'story' is quite another. As a subject a landscape may be attributable to a particular date or period on the evidence of its content, what it actually shows (e.g. a panorama of London before or after the Great Fire of 1666); whereas in dating a landscape painting as a work of art many other kinds of evidence (e.g. artistic style, brushwork or the materials used), may be invoked as well as its content.

Even more tiresome can be the difficulty of placing a landscape painting in its spatial context. Landscapes display a vast range of topographical particularity which we may think of as a continuum from precise, imitative representations at one pole through imaginary landscapes to abstractions at the other. Some paintings, for instance, like Canaletto's townscapes or Kip's bird's-eye views of the great English parks and mansions, are clearly intended to be accurate representations of their subjects; but many landscape painters had no such intentions. 'Artist's licence' may be employed for a variety of reasons. Gilpin, for instance, often exaggerated sublime features in his drawings to achieve a greater dramatic effect and was followed in this practice by most painters of the Romantic era. Some of the early descriptions of Australia – pictorial and literary – were intended to persuade would-be settlers to emigrate, and in such a case the accurate portrayal of topographical detail was of secondary importance and might indeed be counter-productive. In a recent paper, Michael Pidgley (1983) showed that buildings of unique and unmistakable design, which had been successfully used in one painting, were re-engaged to serve in others, each painting being designated by a very specific but quite different place name!

Very often, however, landscape paintings have no locational attribution at all. Almost all the paintings of Claude Lorrain can be seen to owe something to the landscapes of Apennine Italy, but they became almost 'placeless' models for a kind of universal, idyllic landscape style. The geographical authenticity of their *personalities* was not important, and they could therefore be made up – 'composed' – of parts taken, as it were, from stock and assembled in any number of pleasing arrangements.

Once the idea of putting together components drawn from different origins is accepted, the way lies open to every kind of compositional possibility. The imagination is no longer constrained by geographical authenticity or even plausibility. Incongruity of association may become almost an objective, as it was in the landscapes of Surrealism. This kind of art may tell us little about what the real world is like, but a great deal about how we perceive it. But in all fantasy landscapes, from Hieronymus

Bosch to Tolkien, there is a fairly solid loyalty to the representation of the *parts*, even if the whole is incongruous to the point of
absurdity.

The recognition that there may be a big gap between the world
as it is, and the world as it is perceived to be by the artist, raises one
of the most difficult problems in assimilating into scientific
research raw material drawn from the arts, namely the balance
between subjectivity and objectivity. An individual artist is not
necessarily (or even probably) a very trustworthy guide to a
society's *general* habits of perception. Certainly there is a sense
in which the artist may conceive it to be his role to 'hold up a
mirror to the times', but invariably he seeks to reflect life *as he
sees it*. The greatest artists have neither been very good at, nor
very interested in, suppressing their own individuality, and
the researcher seeking objectivity may well experience difficulty in knowing how to handle information processed sub-
jectively by individualistic, often unorthodox, and even eccentric
minds.

Another problem area concerns conflict of interpretation. Here
again the arts have no monopoly. Scientific progress has always
been stimulated, often even precipitated, by conflict and controversy, but one usually has the feeling that, underlying this
conflict, there is a belief that there must be a 'right' answer which
the diligent may discover, provided they adhere rigidly to the
rules of the game. Art critics (and art historians), on the other
hand, seem to have a lower expectation of discovering a 'correct'
view of many of the issues which they study. After all, they have
no way of proving the values which they attach to their subject
matter. The best they can hope for is a consensus view, and even
that is likely to be mistrusted, unless it is a consensus of the right
people; which means, as often as not, the people who agree with
them. Disagreement, unresolved conflict and the open mind seem
to be more acceptable in the arts as facts of academic and
professional life, and it is understandable that this attitude may
be as irritating to a scientist as is agnosticism to an orthodox
theologian. How can you argue with people who don't know
their own minds?

Aesthetic values and fashions

The great changes in landscape design in 18th-century England,
for instance, accompanied philosophical arguments about aesthetic values which cannot be said ever to have been conclusively

resolved. The fact that landowners in the middle of the century employed 'improvers' to design landscapes according to the very opposite principles to those which had prevailed when the century began did not mean that these improvers had suddenly discovered the truth – that André le Nôtre had got it all wrong and that enlightened posterity would never make the same mistake again. It meant simply that society had generally espoused a fashion which rejected the style of its grandfathers, many characteristics of which were destined to be revived by its grandchildren. The straight avenue, the formal garden, the qualities of regularity and symmetry and other manifestations of order all returned under Queen Victoria, albeit in different forms and guises, together with a renewed admiration for those great masterpieces, like Versailles, Vaux-le-Viscomte and even Hampton Court, which had managed to survive the zeal of the improvers. A temporary change in the consensus view of what makes an attractive landscape is very different from the discovery of some new aesthetic principle of universal and perpetual validity, yet one has only to read what has been written by architectural critics over the past few decades to realise that the difference is not invariably understood.

Such changes of fashion may occur in the sciences, for instance in medicine, where the abandonment of one kind of treatment in favour of another may be followed by a return to the *status quo ante*. However, they are more commonplace in the arts, and when scientists first encounter them in the context of the arts, they may experience considerable difficulty in knowing how to handle them. Thus the early attempts at quantitative landscape evaluation, by supposedly scientific methods, were based on far too simplistic assumptions about correlations between landscape components – such as mountains, trees and water – and the capacity of these features invariably to evoke the same aesthetic responses. The use of 'surrogates' in landscape evaluation is based on just such an assumption which, among other things, minimises the importance of composition as a determinant of aesthetic response and begs some very important questions, not least in the light of the emphasis laid on compositional arrangements by art critics and historians at all periods. The surrogate, in short, was accorded scientific respectability on the flimsiest of credentials. Had its references been taken up with those scholars who were familiar with the fickle vicissitudes of landscape taste, as recorded in the artistic heritage of the world's civilisations, they might have been able to give a warning about the dangers of placing too much credence on the reliability of the new recruit.

Symbolic meanings and values

The surrogate is a type of symbol, and I suspect that the arts, which have been involved with the study of symbolism much longer than the sciences, may have lessons to teach about this immensely complex subject which we would all ignore at our peril. Symbolism is perhaps the single most important link between students of landscape in the arts and the sciences. It is concerned with the meanings of what we perceive – more specifically those meanings that lie behind an object or an act, rather than those that are an intrinsic part of it. It so happened that the environmental psychologists became seriously interested in symbolism at a time when scholars in the arts were also displaying a new awareness of the importance of the *content*, as opposed to the techniques, of art and to the meanings attached to that content. The stories and messages of pictures, their iconography and their significance as statements of ideas have been prominent subjects of discussion in recent years. Much of this discussion has been directed towards historical and social messages. However, it is increasingly recognised that landscape, even in paintings whose message is primarily historical or cultural, religious or psychological, is much more than mere wallpaper, arbitrarily related to the events, objects or arrangements which may ostensibly be the subject of the work.

Symbolic meaning is often communicated by objects which are consistently associated with particular ideas over long periods of time. For instance, the association of evergreen trees and shrubs with eternal life goes back a long way before Spenser's 'cypress funeral'. Already, in classical literature, the cypress was sacred to Pluto, god of the underworld. There are many other symbolic associations of long standing which have important implications for landscape. For example, elevated places often have significance for religious ceremonies of all sorts. The highly complex symbolism of ancient 'ley lines' is still being worked out. Water symbolism, which is of great antiquity, endows rivers, lakes and fountains with special religious values, while more dramatic expressions of the powers of nature, such as may be found in volcanic activity, have almost invariably invited some symbolic interpretation of an animistic kind, and much of this is recorded in the arts.

Changing attitudes to landscape can often best be interpreted in symbolic terms. The great 18th-century revolution in landscape architecture, already referred to, provides an example. The landscape designs of André le Nôtre can be seen as a kind of

victory parade to celebrate the triumph of aristocratic, landowning man over nature (as well as over the lower orders of
society). But before the mid-18th century the English aristocracy
had become sufficiently sure of itself to relinquish the image of
nature as a conquered enemy and to seek to reinstate her as an
equal partner. Nowhere is this change of policy better expressed
than in Pope's *Epistle to Lord Burlington* (1731). Though ostensibly
a moral essay against 'false taste', it concentrates particularly on
extravagant methods of landscaping in furtherance of what the
poet conceives to be the wrong aesthetic objectives.

Often the symbolic association is not so much with the
particular objects as with the environmental arrangements suggestive of behavioural opportunities. Concepts like 'territoriality'
and 'personal space', which figure prominently in the literature of
psychology, find expression in the distribution as well as in the
intrinsic properties of environmental objects. Thus great symbolic importance may attach to the contrast between open and
confined space, to the advantages of elevated ground and of
implied opportunities for movement along paths and over
bridges, to the disadvantages suggested by impediments like
walls, fences or unbridged rivers. In short, to positive and
negative strategic values expressed in terms of voids and masses,
slopes and breaks of slope, the distribution of land and water
surfaces, and so on. All these concepts found their way into
landscape painting centuries before they were taken on board by
the environment psychologists.

Dimensions of 'The Arts'

If my references to 'The Arts' have so far presented a picture of a
single homogeneous body of human experience clearly distin-
guishable from the sciences, this is far from the truth. The arts
themselves comprise many forms and many media, each one of
which has its own peculiar problems. Pictorial and literary
descriptions of the same area, for instance, inevitably differ in
their emphasis, in their presentation of information, and in their
capacity to provide the basis for mental reconstruction of the
original.

Some attempts have been made to study landscape descriptions
in different media and to identify the linking mechanisms
between them. For example, Karl Kroeber (1972) compared
Constable's painting *The Cornfield* with Wordsworth's poem,
Tintern Abbey; but I believe that Kroeber's observation, 'Possibly

we should be humble enough to recognize that in our comparisons between the arts we have not advanced far enough to
establish genuinely systematic approaches' (p. 76) still holds true.

In a publication of the same year, John Barrell (1972) encountered the problem in a somewhat different form when discussing
the controversy about the way in which we generally perceive
Claude's landscapes. He challenged the usual assertion that the
eye falls first on objects in the foreground, then in the middle
ground, and gradually proceeds to the distant horizon which is its
ultimate goal. In fact, he says, this progression takes place only
after an initial act of observation which encompasses a broad,
general view of the distant landscape.

This is obviously a difficult hypothesis to test experimentally,
but Barrell points to strong circumstantial evidence by reference
to 18th-century poets, especially Thomson, who regularly describes prospects from high vantage points precisely by Barrell's
formula. The painter presents all his or her information at once
and the observer may pick it up in whatever order he or she
chooses, but the poet cannot escape the necessity of arranging it in
some particular narrative sequence which becomes fixed when he
or she writes the poem. In this way the services of one medium of
presentation are enlisted to throw light on the way we perceive
landscapes through another. In a recent publication Prince (1984)
has shown how advantageous it is to geographers if they study
landscape through paintings, while Howard (1984) has placed
the emphasis the other way round and demonstrated that the
application of geographical techniques can make some quite
dramatic contributions to the study of art history.

Once we begin to recognise that different art forms or different
media have different characteristics of this sort we may re-think
certain assumptions which tend to condition our view of
landscape art. For instance, considering the phenomenon of
'serial vision' (experiencing different landscapes in chronological
succession), we may find that the normal categorisation of art
forms into the visual and literary arts does not hold good. Instead,
if we group together those forms which allow the artist to employ
serial vision and those which do not, we shall find ourselves
detaching motion-pictures from the other visual arts like painting
and still photography and putting them in the same group as the
literary arts.

Other 'inter-media' problems of this sort still await serious
study. Consider, for instance, how many composers have used
the names of places or landscape types as the titles of musical
compositions. If we feel that these 'fit' – that there really is some

affinity between Karelia and Sibelius' composition of that name – there must be some rational basis for the connection, even if it is only an association formed by expectation, if, that is to say, the idea of the place has been put into our minds by the title before the musical experience begins. Most people, however, would feel that there is more in it than that, even if we are still a long way from understanding the mechanism by which this kind of linkage may be achieved.

Integrating the arts and sciences in landscape research

If, then, students of landscape have difficulty in bridging these gaps within the arts we can scarcely be surprised that they have not made more progress in bridging the gaps between the arts and the sciences. What has already been achieved points to the possibility of establishing all kinds of meaningful correlations. Thornes (1978, 1984), for instance, has had considerable success in explaining some of the relationships between paintings and meteorological phenomena. Paulson (1982) has begun to develop the idea that the compositional structure of landscapes as paintings may consistently reflect common geological bases. But these investigations are to be seen as signposts towards a vast unexplored area with innumerable opportunities for further work.

I suggest, then, that those who approach the study of landscape from a scientific background will do themselves, and their work, a great disservice if they are not prepared to approach the arts in a spirit of optimistic expectation, attempting to discover therein opportunities to extend their experience of landscape beyond the limits of their own specialised interests. In return, those who seek to introduce ideas from the arts into the landscape debate have no right, and should have no desire, to expect them to be accorded a role, a status or an authority which cannot be vindicated. They should also recognise the ambivalences and the contradictions to be found in the arts which may, for instance, be both innovatory and conservative. They can stimulate new ideas, new meanings and new values, but they can also fossilise old ones.

If we are to make real progress in furthering not only the co-existence but also the integration of the arts and the sciences in landscape research we should familiarise ourselves with the widest possible range of landscape experience. This does not mean that we should use each part of it in a similar way, but rather that, by building for ourselves as wide a framework of understanding as we can, we shall be the better able to recognise both the potentialities and the limitations of each piece of the picture.

At present I believe we are too ready to settle for an involvement with those parts of the whole which fall within our own field of expertise. Our task is nothing less than to create a new field in which we must be prepared not, of course, to abandon our own special interests, but to make a real effort to see them in a new and broader perspective.

It is in this context that I think even the most scientific of us should be open-minded enough to regard the arts as a potential source of quite different kinds of insight affording us a grasp of the truth which no passage of scientific prose can awaken. We may not all find such insight in the same things. The poem by Norman Nicholson, which does a lot for me, may do nothing at all for another student of landscape; but if any of us is disposed to exclude it from our consideration, even from our researches, simply on the grounds that it is not 'science' but only 'art', then perhaps we are revealing more about our own limitations than about those of Norman Nicholson; and perhaps we ought to do something about it.

References

Barrell, J. 1972. *The idea of landscape and the sense of place, 1730–1840: an approach to the poetry of John Clare*. Cambridge: Cambridge University Press.

Howard, P. 1984. Change in the landscape perception of artists. *Landscape Research* **9**(3), 41–4.

Kroeber, K. 1972. *Tintern Abbey* and *The Cornfield*: serendipity as a method of inter-media criticism. *Journal of Aesthetics and Art Criticism* **31**, 67–77.

Lowenthal, D. and H. Prince 1965. English landscape tastes. *Geographical Review* **55**, 186–222.

Nicholson, N. 1981. 'Beck' in *Sea to the west*. London: Faber and Faber.

Paulson, R. 1982. *Literary landscapes: Turner and Constable*. New Haven and London: Yale University Press.

Pidgley, M. 1983. *Landscape titles and artistic licence*. Paper delivered to the Conference on Landscape and Painting, Landscape Research Group *et al.*, Exeter, October, 1983.

Pope, A. 1731. *An epistle to the Right Honourable Richard Earl of Burlington, Etc.* ('*Of false taste*'). London: Gulliver.

Prince, H. 1984. Landscape through painting. *Geography* **69**, 3–18.

Thornes, J. E. 1978. *The accurate dating of John Constable's cloud studies, 1821/22 using historical weather records*. London: Department of Geography, University College.

Thornes, J. E. 1984. A reassessment of the relationship between John Constable's meteorological understanding and his painting of clouds, *Landscape Research* **9**(3), 20–9.

Critiques and queries

The comments below have been selected principally and deliberately from those criticising the position advanced by Jay Appleton. This selection is thus designed to demonstrate the wide
divergence of opinion amongst those involved in the landscape
field.

Dick Watson   This chapter raises some very difficult questions,
and does so in ways that are extremely useful; in general I found
this paper's argument very constructive and encouraging. I like
the use of the forensic parallel, but feel that the contribution
which the arts can make is often more properly directed towards
the affective. It is certainly, however, complementary to the
scientific approach, by first establishing data, secondly establishing alternative possibilities, thirdly, in interpretation, and
finally, in evaluation.

The third of these often involves the fourth, since one can
interpret a work of art in ways which demonstrate its value. But
the final difficulty with 'the arts' is that they are assessing and
discovering the undiscoverable – the human mind in its relationship with that which lies outside it. This is not just *terra
incognita* but *terra imponderabilita*: 'a fool', said Blake, 'sees not the
same tree that a wise man sees'. How many of us are fools, and to
what degree?

The study of the humanities is an endless study of what
Wordsworth called the 'infinite complexity' of the mind and the
external world 'acting and re-acting upon one another'. There
is no stable area upon which to operate, except for the very
elementary cataloguing of constituent data in the external world –
trees, grass, water, etc. The remainder is a shifting sand containing at least three elements: the mind, the external world, and
the relationship between them.

It is possible that a better analogy than the forensic one might be
with medicine: the doctor employs all sorts of diagnostic skills
and tests, but also takes into account the individuality of the
patient, his family circumstances, and so on. Science and human
feeling are complementary.

Ian Brotherton   I am unhappy with the general thesis that
artists and scientists feel mutual unease (p. 26) because they
employ differing methodologies (pp. 30–32). Does not the
unease, if such there be and I am not sure of it, stem from a more
basic misunderstanding of *what* the other is about, not how they

do what they are about? We need clearer indications of the role that each of the arts and sciences can play in landscape research, and what problems and questions concern each discipline.

Stephen Daniels The 'subjective–objective dichotomy' is one of those categorical either/or notions which disables thinking about the arts and sciences, and needs to be scrutinised philosophically before we go ahead and 'handle it scientifically' because we may find that such a dichotomy is untenable in the first place.

The categories 'the Arts' and 'the Sciences' need to be scrutinised no less thoroughly. A fundamental question: is landscape a 'thing' that 'artists' and 'scientists' look at from different viewpoints? This positivist assumption seems to underly this paper: 'Most scholarly disciplines and practical enterprises impinge on *it* (my emphasis) yet virtually nothing is known about landscape as a totality.' If we conceptualise landscape not as a *thing* (we therefore may in principle know *completely*) but as a *way of seeing* then some of our questions will need to be radically rephrased.

We need to specify the social context of artistic and scientific practice. There is a tendency, especially in humanistic geography, to overprivilege the creative facility of the artist. We should reimmerse the artist in the context of his or her time and see them negotiating the restraints and possibilities of medium, compositional form, the climate of ideas, patronage, audience, display, the look and organisation of real places. We might also raise the issue of ideology and image making.

Andrew Gilg Appleton's paper makes the very good point that we should concentrate on the process of seeing à la Barrell. However, I think the art/science conflict is overplayed, and I take it to be self-evident that the two approaches are vitally necessary in landscape studies.

Ewart Johns In response to the general thrust of all the questions raised by this paper, I think we should start by drawing a distinction, on the arts side, between those who practice (in either fine art or design) and those who write as critics, historians or philosophers. The former are under-represented in landscape research and could be called on for their opinions with benefit. An artist who trusts to his or her instincts (which are subjected to just as much rigour in the execution of a work as are scientific researches, although a rigour of a different kind), can act as an essential 'sounding board' for theoretical ideas. In other words, *'vive la différence'*!

Muriel Laverack Even the small collation of papers here shows the acceptance of a wide range of disciplines as being relevant, spanning arts and science. Long may it continue – not too much integration, please.

Indeed, is there a gulf which matters between arts and sciences regarding landscape? Scientific techniques may be applied to resolve, say, a geological issue and the geologist will be satisfied with an answer which is valid in his or her terms. A romantic or 'arts' view of the same landscape does not necessarily relate to the geological answer, nor does the geologist dispute the romantic view on the basis that there is a bigger wave-cut platform or whatever elsewhere. Neither view is decisive in ranking the landscape. Geology is but one factor, while it is Constable's paintings of East Anglia, not necessarily the landscape itself, which are sublime.

Sue Clifford There seems to be a tendency to want to pillage the arts for science's sake and to use art as artefact (paintings, books, murals). But we have several generations of many kinds of artists all around us, who are preoccupied by and inspired by nature, landscape and place. Will they lead landscape taste into the 21st century? Do we know how they use/translate their emotions? Why they can express them? What can be learnt from their lack of inhibition, their 'expertise', their myriad vocabularies? Rather than pillaging past paintings . . . why not look at living painters. What do we have to learn from their use of metaphors/symbolism?

The papers in this collection are very academically biased. What of the pragmatic need (for some of us) to care for landscape? What values and meanings are involved in conservation? How useful can this debate be for practical action?

Jay Appleton replies: As a committed advocate of a liaison between the arts and the sciences I wish I could believe that the differences in their methodologies need not cause us concern. I do *not* want to see us all becoming the same; it is the meeting of disparate minds that makes an organisation like the Landscape Research Group tick. I *do* want to see us all working within a common framework which can accommodate very different styles, methodologies and approaches.

When I find art historians arguing, not that the evidence of a scientist is invalid and should therefore not be believed, but that it is irrelevant and therefore should not be heard, this worries me. I am equally unhappy when, as an external examiner, I have to defend a candidate who has been marked down by a teacher with a 'science background' on the grounds that a thesis cannot be regarded as 'scientific' if its author draws on the works of Shelley. This is the context of my plea that we should carefully re-examine our several techniques, methodologies and even attitudes in the hope that we may work most effectively in the furtherance of our common interests.

4 *Psychological reflections on landscape*

KENNETH H. CRAIK

After 15 years of intermittent inquiry into human responsiveness to landscape (Craik 1968, 1972a,b, 1975; Craik & Feimer 1979; Feimer *et al.* 1981) the opportunity here to offer some personal reflections on one's approach to the topic is very welcome.

Much of the research in environmental psychology pertinent to landscape has dealt with environmental perception and environmental experience. However, a specific focus upon landscape meanings and values pushes the agenda usefully into new areas of investigation. Within psychology it broadens our concerns to include cognition and personality.

To illustrate briefly the kinds of questions addressed by environmental psychologists, I will discuss three sets of issues and then point to promising lines of future research. These themes are, first, landscape perception and landscape experience, secondly, landscape cognition and landscape meanings, and finally, personality and landscape values.

Landscape perception and landscape experience

The immediate, here-and-now, on-site impressions of landscape experienced by persons seem to me to embody the central psychological issues of landscape research, either directly or indirectly. Landscape itself I take to be a human phenomenon, an emergent of the interplay between the observer, on the one hand, and landform and land use on the other.

First, the experience of a particular landscape depends upon the characteristics of the observer. Do the fool and the wise man see the same tree? How do the background and prior personal environments of the observer affect perceptions of a specific setting? How do newcomers and natives differ in their perceptions of a landscape? How does professional training of one sort or another influence or shape landscape perception?

Secondly, the transaction between the observer and the physical setting – that is, the context in which the observer encounters the here-and-now place – is important. Do observers explicitly or implicitly instruct themselves to pay attention to certain aspects of a setting, such as its botanical characteristics, or its aesthetic features, or its historical referents? What environmental role is the observer enacting? Is it, for example, that of observer of picturesque landscapes, or that of professional landscape evaluator, or that of Sierra Club backpacker? By what medium of presentation is the setting conveyed to the observer? Is it by means of direct on-site visits, by photograph or film, by artistic sketch or literary portrait?

Thirdly, in seeking to understand landscape perceptions and experiences, even psychologists enjoy no magical access to the minds of others. Thus, a question of importance is the particular format of response used by the observer in communicating landscape perceptions, such as open-ended free reports or more structured adjective checklists and rating scales. Last but not least – simply the biased sequencing of a psychologist – comes the important influence of landform and land use patterns in shaping landscape perceptions.

This framework within environmental psychology has generated a lively international research program (Daniel & Vining 1983; Feimer 1983; Zube et al. 1982). Yet it must be stressed that the answers to these questions are far from having been settled and in most instances the questions themselves have not yet been fully or adequately formulated.

On the observer's side, a number of factors can be identified as influencing or accounting for the outcome of landscape impression-formation processes, as Fig. 4.1 indicates. Everyday perception is an active process, guided by psychological sets and

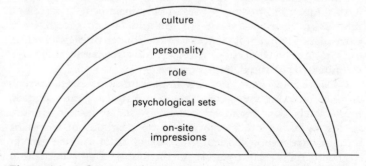

Figure 4.1   Influences in the perception process (from Craik 1983a).

other cognitive processes. Persons encounter landscape settings with something like a plan to attend to and process certain kinds of information about it. As Leff and Gordon (1980) and their associates at the University of Vermont have shown, persons can be instructed to take these cognitive sets intentionally and report upon their difficulty, complexity, and pleasurableness. For example, to attend to the shapes, lines, colours and textures of a landscape scene is relatively difficult for university students; to attend to imagining changes that would make the scene better is relatively pleasant. In everyday life, of course, these cognitive sets are seldom so intentional or explicit and are instead organised around psychological factors, such as the role the person is enacting at the time or the individual's personality dispositions.

I continue to be disappointed that the construct of environmental role has not received greater research attention. Elsewhere (Craik 1970, 1983a) I have illustrated how the constructs of role expectations, role acquisition, role enactment, and role skill can be marshalled to delineate and understand the role of observer of picturesque landscapes. A taxonomy of scenic roles (e.g. the role of observer of romantic landscape; the role of wilderness user) could be developed that encompasses historical as well as contemporary roles.

At a further level of analysis, the roles an individual elects to enact reflect or give expression to more enduring personality characteristics. And the roles available to an individual are a function of cultural forces. Variations on the role of tourist are beginning to receive historical and sociological examination (Cohen 1972, MacCannell 1973) and to be recognised as having consequential impacts upon host cultures and environments (Hawkins et al. 1980).

An intriguing question related to landscape meanings and values is whether the experience of landscape qua landscape is itself a function of cognitive set or role enactment. To get to a meeting in Harrow-on-the-Hill on time or to search for a particular restaurant off the Kensington Road may focus attention on a task or specific structure and away from the larger environmental context that is landscape.

On a journey one can review the nature of landscape experience, based upon how we note the sequential landscapes passing immediately before and around us. A focus upon the entire setting as composition or organisation clearly approximates a sense of landscape experience or perception to a much greater degree than the focus upon any element or selected point within the setting. Furthermore, perceived composition is a focus of experience which one can more or less achieve or ignore, as a function of cognitive set or intention to attend to it rather than to focal elements in the setting. Thus, as one moves through the city or countryside, a continually transformed, not static, compositional experience is at the heart of landscape perception. (This formulation is due in part to an extended conversation with Ewart Johns held during a journey from the Royal Institution on Albemarle Street, London to Down Hall at Hatfield Heath, Bishop's Stortford, Herts, on 4 April 1984.) In this way, the organisational nature of landscape perception serves as a counterpart to the physical composition of spaces on the land, which Brinck Jackson has highlighted as the central notion of 'actual' landscape (Jackson, 1986).

Given this analysis, a specific psychological question arises: under what conditions do lay persons in their daily rounds experience and appreciate landscape *qua* landscape? That is, when are they cognitively set to attend to compositional facets of their physical surrounds? The nature and prevalence of such conditions must affect the meaning and value which landscapes hold for them.

In the study of landscape experience and perception environmental psychologists take as their subject matter not the landscape itself in its physical status, or as natural processes, land management practices, or historically evolving forms, but instead the experiences and perceptions of other individuals. In a sense, we study landscape as hearsay or rumour. This mode of inquiry not only places the burden of yet another meaning upon the term 'landscape' but also represents a type of investigation quite distinct from many other forms of landscape research. Furthermore, environmental psychologists declare the landscape perceptions and experiences of all persons to be of potential scientific interest, including those of the ordinary person. I anticipate that it may be more difficult for most experts in landscape to maintain a similar span of interest. It is rather like asking enologists and professional winetasters to remain fascinated with the open-ended description and judgements of bouquet, colour, aroma, acidity, etc. made by recent initiates to the pleasures of wine.

Landscape cognition and landscape meaning

Within environmental psychology, a more recent research interest shifts the focus of attention away from our immediate here-and-now experience of specific settings and begins to

examine the question of how we represent landscapes cognitively
and how we think about landscapes (Ward & Russell 1981).

Cognitive categories

Individuals categorise physical landform and land use patterns by
the use of concepts such as 'mountain', 'seashore', and 'meadow'.
Some also employ such differentiating constructs as 'a Devon
landscape' or a 'Mendocino landscape'. Clearly, individuals vary
in the nature and complexity of their environmental category
systems, but in what ways they do so has not yet been carefully
mapped.

The recent contributions of Rosch and others in cognitive
psychology (Rosch 1975, 1978; Tversky & Hemenway 1983)
may be useful in exploring judgements of prototypical versus
peripheral members of important environmental cognitive categories. Cognitive categories such as nature (Wohlwill 1983),
technology, and landscape might also be analysed in this fashion,
as well as the concept of environmental quality (Craik & Zube
1976).

How we judge the fittingness of an introduced structure or
element in a setting probably depends upon our environmental
construct system. For example, Groat (1983) has begun to
examine the differing ways in which a new building in the urban
landscape may be deemed contextually suitable. One structure
may seek to replicate the existing site organisation and the
architectural style of contiguous buildings. Another structure
may attempt to highlight the architectural vocabulary of a region
while ignoring immediately adjacent buildings. In each case, the
judgement of fittingness depends upon observers who possess the
cognitive categories required to abstract certain features of a
structure and to link them to comparable but not identical features
of nearby or widely dispersed structures. The use of environmental simulation to vary building and surrounding site features
systematically, combined with the application of techniques of
cognitive psychology, could advance our understanding of con-
textual properties that may be central to our notion of landscape, both urban and natural (Groat 1983; Wohlwill 1979).

Environmental inferences

Cognition also becomes relevant in analysing the inferences we
make about the environment. For example, in urban settings
we often attempt to use our diagnostic ability with regard to

restaurants. How accurately do we make inferences about the interiors of restaurants (e.g. the length of the menu; the price of a steak) based upon the exterior (e.g. the presence of a neon sign; a brass rail on the window)? Which of these many cues afforded by the exterior facade and signing do we use; which ones should we use (that is, which have predictive validity); and, how accurate are our overall estimates?

The same diagnostic capacities are active in our encounters with the countryside, of course. Psychological research techniques are available to explore these questions of environmental interpretation as they apply to ordinary persons (Brunswik 1956, Craik & Appleyard 1980, Craik 1981). They can also be used to document and analyse expert judgement processes and have been applied to understand how radiologists judge gastric ulcer conditions from X-rays (Slovic *et al.* 1971) and how stockbrokers judge potential for capital appreciation of business firms from portfolios (Slovic *et al.* 1972). The comparable diagnostic abilities of landscape architects, land agents and other experts in interpreting the countryside have not been systematically documented in this way. I believe studies of this kind would show that their skills are generally under-rated by themselves and by others.

The communication model of environmental meaning

The analyses of how we 'read' the text of the environment have treated environmental meaning as a one-way exchange. However, it can also be approached as a two-way form of communication. Donald Appleyard, my late colleague at Berkeley, formulated the issue of environmental meaning as a communication process. Adopting a model from the linguist and philosopher Roman Jakobson (1960), he employed it flexibly to serve many purposes. In his analysis of the planning review process (Appleyard 1976, 1977), the proponents of a project communicate what is planned by way of various simulation media to an audience that includes review commissions, the general public, etc., and then receive feedback from these evaluators. In his analysis of the home (Appleyard 1979a), the owner communicates messages about the self, personal taste, etc. to neighbours and others through the character and appearance of the house, and then receives various forms of social feedback.

In an important generalisation regarding environmental actions and symbols, Appleyard (1979c) viewed the physical environment itself as a social or political phenomenon embodying the intentions of the original initiators or the current maintaining agents. These messages communicated by the physical environment, in his view, convey not merely knowledge about environmental identity and structure, but also claims of social group or personal identity. Appleyard primarily applied this communication model rather than stopping to analyse explicitly its conceptual implications and possibilities. However, in his later works, he did begin to address the issues of the power to control and participate in the process and the question of how that power is distributed, negotiated or fought over by social groups and individuals (Appleyard 1979b, 1981). Further attention to Appleyard's communication model of environmental meaning promises to be an important avenue to advances on this topic.

Personality and landscape values

A psychologist approaches the issue of landscape values not from the position of cultural consensus and normative pattern, but instead from the recognition of readily demonstrated individual pluralism (Craik 1975, 1976; Little, in press).

While some people display an awareness of landscapes and clearly prize, treasure and cherish the countryside, others show a lack of sensitivity to landscape and appear to appreciate it to a lesser extent. Indeed, our research finds substantial variation among individuals on certain general orientations or dispositions toward the environment, such as pastoralism, urbanism, antiquarianism, environmental trust and stimulus seeking (McKechnie 1974, 1977). In addition, individuals vary systematically in their 'worldviews' concerning a set of contemporary policy issues that bear upon development, technology, preservation, population, rationality of decision making, and centralisation of decision making (Buss & Craik 1983; Buss *et al*. in press).

Contemporary Worldview 'A' embodies the notion of a high growth, high technology, centralised free enterprise society, with a pro-business stance on regulation, materialistic goals, and rational, quantified decision-making processes. Contemporary Worldview 'B' stresses levelling off material and technological growth, concern about social and environmental impacts of growth, redistribution of resources from richer to poorer nations, lower levels of consumption, decentralisation of both control and population, goals of human self-realisation, and participative decision making guided by non-materialistic values.

Although specific landscapes are a function of the immediate, on-site experiences of observers, issues of landscape change and preservation can be located within the broader on-going process of societal discourse and decision. Often the other side of the coin of environmental impact is technological application. Thus the relevance of contemporary worldviews to issues of landscape is clear. How specifically the Contemporary Worldviews 'A' and 'B' which we have assessed relate to individuals' everyday experience of landscape, and the values they ascribe to it, is an important matter for future research.

Another important source of landscape values can be found in personal environmental histories, as revealed by autobiographical accounts. These highly distinctive personalised affective ties and memories make one individual's muddy little cove another person's inestimably valuable and prized childhood vacation spot. The techniques of personality assessment and research make it possible to explore the individual level of analysis as an important avenue to an understanding of the genesis of landscape values (Craik 1976). The assessment of individual variations in personal background, environmental dispositions and contemporary worldviews provides the means of examining the influence of more or less enduring personality characteristics upon the experience of landscape and policy stances toward it.

I have also been curious about the relation of a more familiar variable – namely liberalism–conservatism – to landscape. In a study conducted in Marin County, California (Craik 1983b), we took a sample of residents on a nine mile tour through an area of their county. As part of the study, participants also completed a large number of procedures assessing their personality dispositions, attitudes, and background. One of the strongest correlates of degree of preference or liking for the tour area was liberalism–conservatism, as assessed both by self-rating and by Democratic versus Republican party affiliation. Why was conservatism related to liking this particular area, which included a highway, shopping centre, light industrial park and several residential districts, each representing middle-to-high income planned developments? Would the same area be associated with conservatism if located elsewhere, and not in a county that also includes such elite and avant-garde places as Sausalito, Tiburon, Pt. Reyes Station, and Mill Valley? More broadly, what are the general relations between political orientations and landscape meanings and values?

The issue of historic preservation also raises certain unexplored questions regarding personality dispositions. I have long wanted to find the time to study the phenomenon of indigenous historians. If any voluntary organisation survives over a number of years (e.g. a neighbourhood association, a bowling team), a small number of historians of the outfit seem naturally to emerge. What are the personality characteristics of such individuals? Do they share attributes similar to those of individuals actively involved in historic preservation efforts (e.g. members of Save Britain's Heritage; the American National Trust) (Lowenthal 1983, Lowenthal & Binney 1981)? Does McKechnie's Antiquarianism Scale of the Environmental Response Inventory (McKechnie 1974, 1977), assessing a preference for the old versus the modern, offer an effective means of beginning to address this topic? A rich area for psychological research also awaits us here.

Research recommendations

A series of possible studies can be suggested, and my recommendations are considered within the three lines of inquiry previously introduced. They should be seen simply as illustrations of new endeavours that can advance our understanding.

Landscape perception and landscape experience

A neglected topic in environmental psychology is the process by which an individual becomes acquainted with the landscapes of a new region. Acquaintance is not provided instantaneously but rather accrues from continuing exploration and interaction, both focused and incidental. As Lowenthal (1978, p. 385) has noted: 'The context of interaction between man and milieu depends, moreover, on mood and circumstance, weather and light and time of day, views from on foot or in a vehicle, stationary or in motion, deliberately chosen or accidentally come upon.' This process is active, dynamic, perhaps stage-like in its development, but little understood.

As an individual becomes more acquainted with the landscapes of a region, a sense of familiarity with it is claimed. But what is the meaning of familiarity with landscape? Does it refer to mere exposure to the region? Does it refer to claims of knowledge about the region? Does it refer only to well founded and accurate claims to knowledge? Or does it refer to a subjective sense of personal ties to the region? Psychological issues such as the multiple meanings of familiarity would be usefully explored through studies of the acquaintance process and its residues.

Within a research project those sensitive and expert in their perceptions and articulate in expression could make an important contribution through a systematic and organised scheme of depositing log-books and other records for analysis. Those who have relocated their residence or are spending an extended period in a new locale might contribute, using a standard set of timeposts for recording impressions. Free descriptions and impressions could be complemented by more structured ways of eliciting impressions of landscapes (Craik 1971, Craik & Feimer in press). At some later date a more formal research design might study a large number of persons moving to the same new region, with some recording their impressions at the first timepost, some at the second, some at the third, and so forth, to control for repeated use of the response formats and procedure (Beck *et al.* 1973). However, a central depository for individual recordings would provide a useful and important basis for initiating an understanding of this familiarisation process.

Landscape cognition and landscape meaning

The rich and differentiated appreciation that is generally accorded to the English landscape raises the possibility of a new examination of the question of regional landscapes. From a psychological viewpoint, regional landscapes represent a system of cognitive categorisation. Recent theoretical work in cognitive psychology (Rosch 1975, 1978) treats categories as cognitively structured around prototype or central members, with non-prototype members becoming progressively more peripheral to the category. At the fuzzy borders, the array of instances or members of a given category blends into adjacent categories. In a study of this kind, a provisional set of regional landscape categories would be selected for study. A large array of specific landscape scenes would be judged in order to establish prototypical and peripheral instances of each regional landscape category.

The degree of consensus regarding the prototypicality of landscapes can be gauged by several indices, including prototypicality ratings, membership judgement response times, and so forth (Rosch *et al.* 1976). Thus, regional landscape categories can be appraised on the degree of consensus that prevails regarding the prototypicality of membership of specific landscapes within each, the diversity of landscapes that qualify for membership, and so on. Furthermore, those regional landscape categories for which adequate consensus regarding membership obtains can then be studied to determine the distinctive features and attributes of the prototypical landscapes for each category. A research project of this kind would provide a valuable occasion for active collaboration between environmental psychologists and landscape experts.

A further research topic related to these differentiated apprecia-
tions arises with the incorporation into agency procedures of
the psychological assessment of impacts upon landscape (Elsner
& Smardon 1979; Rowe & Chestnut 1983). The structure of
methodological issues in this enterprise is so well delineated that
these questions have become largely technical matters (Craik &
Zube 1976; Craik & Feimer 1979); a substantial empirical research
literature is addressing these issues (Feimer 1983, Zube *et al.*
1982). Nevertheless, much more detailed knowledge is required
concerning the generality of judgements of scenic quality across
observer populations, the psychological effectiveness of environmental simulation techniques, and the physical environmental
correlates and predictors of scenic quality judgements.

Personality and landscape values

An understanding of the landscape of a region entails knowledge
of key environmental agents who manage, tend and shape it.
In-depth studies of the orientations, values and backgrounds of
on-site decision-makers are relatively rare (Craik 1972a, Little in
press).

An intensive interview and discussion programme with land
managers, such as resident land agents and National Trust land
agents, would provide a valuable contribution to this area of
research. Day-long sessions could be organised to include
individual interviews in the morning, covering the land agents'
backgrounds, beliefs and practices, conception of their roles, and
impressions of their local landscapes. Afternoon sessions could be
devoted to group discussions of critical incidents and situations
in land management and appropriate responses to them. The
findings from a series of these sessions would yield a group
portrait tracing the sources of beliefs, values and skills of a
significant and consequential class of environmental agents.

A second project might be devoted to a similar exploration of
the origins and personal significance of landscape values for
individuals who have displayed an unusually strong commitment
to landscape. The procedure could take the form of what is
known as the living-in or 'country house' assessment programme
(Wilson 1948, MacKinnon 1962, Wiggins 1973). In these programmes, groups of approximately ten persons are studied at a
time, over several days, preferably in a secluded residential
setting, by a staff of psychologists with a wide range of techniques
and procedures.

From these diverse vantage points the method provides an assessment of the person's social impact (recorded by staff observers on adjective checklists and other formats), personality traits, early life history factors, patterns of career development, environmental dispositions, intellectual styles, interest patterns, and personal values (Barron 1969, MacKinnon 1962). At our Institute of Personality Assessment and Research in Berkeley, highly effective and outstanding individuals in various fields and endeavours have been assessed, including architects, writers, research scientists, mathematicians, and physicians, as well as special groups such as the 1965 American Mount Everest Expedition team (Buss *et al.* in press). The findings of an assessment programme of this kind would dramatically advance our understanding of the personal sources and significance of landscape appreciation in individuals who have demonstrated exceptional commitment to landscape values. The interview portion of the assessment programme would focus upon childhood environments, early influences and models, later educational factors, and how landscape appreciation links to career histories and avocational pursuits.

Conclusion

Environmental psychology is still a relatively new field of scientific investigation and must remain even more modest than landscape research and practice in its claims.

The study of landscape meanings and values calls for the approaches of many disciplines and lines of inquiry. The topic itself must be unpacked and its various components and facets must be delineated. I have indicated some of the specific ways in which it can be reformulated and examined by psychological research. Even within this more restricted domain, the issues raised cannot be addressed head-on through one or a few decisive investigations. Instead, more modest projects offer strategic and useful probes. A few possibilities have been briefly indicated.

The analysis of persons' landscape meanings and values from a psychological point of view will require interpretive resources drawn from history, geography, anthropology, and landscape art and architecture. None of these fields of inquiry need be seen as competing with, intruding upon, threatening or ultimately replacing any other. They are complementary ways of enriching our understanding of the human meanings and values of landscape.

References

Appleyard, D. 1976. *Planning a pluralistic city: conflicting realities in Ciudad Guayana*. Cambridge, Mass.: MIT Press.

Appleyard, D. 1977. Understanding professional media: Issues, theory, and a research agenda. In *Human behavior and environment: advances in theory and research,* I. Altman and J. F. Wohlwill (eds), Volume 2, pp. 47–8. New York: Plenum Press.

Appleyard, D. 1979a. Home. *Architectural Association Quarterly* **2**, 4–20.

Appleyard, D. 1979b. Introduction. In *The conservation of European cities*, D. Appleyard (ed.). Cambridge, Mass.: MIT Press.

Appleyard, D. 1979c. The environment as social symbol: Within a theory of environmental action and perception. *Journal of the American Planning Association* **45**, 143–53.

Appleyard, D. 1981. Identity, power and place. Berkeley, California: University of California, unpublished manuscript.

Barron, F. 1969. *The creative person and creative process*. New York: Holt, Rinehart and Winston.

Beck, R., S. Cohen, K. H. Craik, M. Dwyer, G. McCleary and S. Wapner 1973. Studying environmental moves: A research note. *Environment and Behavior* **5**, 335–49.

Brunswik, E. 1956. *Perception and the representative design of psychological experiments* 2nd edn. Berkeley, California: University of California Press.

Buss, D. M. and K. H. Craik 1983. Contemporary worldviews: personal and policy implications. *Journal of Applied Social Psychology* **13**, 250–80.

Buss, D. M., K. H. Craik, and K. M. Drake (in press). Contemporary worldviews and perception of the technological system. In *Risk evaluation and management: The social and behavioral sciences*, V. Covello and J. Menkes (eds). New York: Plenum Press.

Cohen, E. 1972. Toward a sociology on international tourism. *Social Research* **39**, 164–82.

Craik, K. H. 1968. The comprehension of the everyday physical environment. *Journal of the American Institute of Planners* **34**, 29–37.

Craik, K. H. 1970. Environmental psychology. In *New directions in psychology 4*. K. H. Craik, *et al.*, pp. 1–122. New York: Holt, Rinehart and Winston.

Craik, K. H. 1971. The assessment of places. In *Advances in psychological assessment,* P. McReynolds, (ed.), Vol. 2, pp. 40–62. Palo Alto, California: Science and Behavior Books.

Craik, K. H. 1972a. Appraising the objectivity of landscape dimensions. In *Natural environments: Studies in theoretical and applied analysis*, J. V. Krutilla (ed.), pp. 292–346. Baltimore, Md.: Johns Hopkins University Press.

Craik, K. H. 1972b. Psychological factors in landscape appraisal. *Environment and Behaviour* **4**, 255–66.

Craik, K. H. 1975. Individual variations in landscape description. In

Landscape assessment: values, perceptions and resources, E. H. Zube, R. O. Brush and J. Fabos (eds), 130–50. Stroudsburg, Pa.: Dowden, Hutchinson and Ross.

Craik, K. H. 1976. The personality research paradigm in environmental psychology. In *Experiencing environments*, S. Wapner, S. Cohen, and B. Kaplan (eds), 55–80. New York: Plenum Press.

Craik, K. H. 1981. Comments on 'The psychological representation of molar physical environments' by Ward and Russell. *Journal of Experimental Psychology: General* **110**, 158–62.

Craik, K. H. 1983a. A role theoretic analysis of scenic quality judgments. In *Managing air quality and scenic quality resources at national parks and wilderness areas*, R. D. Rowe, and L. G. Chestnut (eds), 117–26. Boulder, Co: Westview Press.

Craik, K. H. 1983b. The psychology of the large-scale environment. In *Environmental psychology: directions and perspectives*, N. R. Feimer and E. S. Geller (eds), 67–105. New York: Praeger.

Craik, K. H. and D. Appleyard 1980. Streets of San Francisco: Brunswik's lens model applied to urban inference and assessment. *Journal of Social Issues* **36**, 72–85.

Craik, K. H. and N. R. Feimer 1979. Setting technical standards for visual assessment procedures. In *Our national landscape*, G. Elsner, and R. C. Smardon (eds), 93–100. Berkeley, California: US Forest Service.

Craik, K. H. and N. R. Feimer in press. Environmental assessment. In *Handbook of environmental psychology*, D. Stokols and I. Altman (eds). New York: Wiley.

Craik, K. H. and E. H. Zube (eds) 1976. *Perceiving environmental quality: research and application*. New York: Plenum Press.

Daniel, T. C., and J. Vining 1983. Methodological issues in the assessment of landscape quality. In *Human behavior and environment*, I. Altman and J. F. Wohlwill (eds), Vol. 6, 39–84. New York: Plenum Press.

Elsner, G. H. and R. C. Smardon (eds) 1979. *Our national landscape: A conference on applied techniques for analysis and management of the visual resource*. Berkeley, California: US Forest Service.

Feimer, N. R. 1983. Environmental perception and cognition in rural contexts. In *Rural psychology*, A. W. Childs and G. B. Melton (eds). New York: Plenum Press.

Feimer, N. R., R. C. Smardon and K. H. Craik 1981. Evaluating the effectiveness of observer-based visual resource and impact assessment methods. *Landscape Research* **6**, 12–16.

Groat, L. 1983. Measuring the fit of new to old: A checklist resulting from a study of contextualism. *Architecture* November, 58–61.

Hawkins, D. E., E. L. Shafer and J. M. Rovelstad 1980. *International symposium on tourism and the next decade: Summary and recommendations*. Washington, DC: Georgetown University.

Jackson, J. B. 1986. The vernacular landscape. In *Landscape meanings and values*, E. C. Penning-Rowsell and D. Lowenthal (eds), 65–76. London: Allen & Unwin.

Jakobson, R. 1960. Closing statement: Linguistics and poetics. In *Style in language*, T. A. Sebeck (ed.), 350–77. Cambridge, Mass: MIT Press.

Leff, H. L. and L. R. Gordon 1980. Environmental cognitive sets: A longitudinal study. *Environment and Behavior* 12, 291–328.

Little, B. R. in press. Personality and the environment. In *Handbook of environmental psychology*, D. Stokols and I. Altman (eds). New York: Wiley.

Lowenthal, D. 1978. Finding valued landscapes. *Progress in Human Geography* 2, 373–418.

Lowenthal, D. 1983. Conserving the heritage: Anglo-American comparisons. In *The expanding city*, J. Patten (ed.), pp. 226–76. New York: Academic Press.

Lowenthal, D. and M. Binney (eds) 1981. *Our past before us: Why do we save it?* London: Temple Smith.

MacCannell, D. 1973. Staged authenticity; Arrangements of social space in tourist settings. *American Journal of Sociology* 79, 589–603.

MacKinnon, D. W. 1962. The nature and nurture of creative talent. *American Psychologist* 17, 484–95.

McKechnie, G. E. 1974. *Manual for the Environmental Response Inventory*. Palo Alto, California: Consulting Psychologists' Press.

McKechnie, G. E. 1977. The Environmental Response Inventory in application. *Environment and Behavior* 9, 255–76.

Rosch, E. 1975. Cognitive representations of semantic categories. *Journal of Experimental Psychology: General* 104, 192–233.

Rosch, E. 1978. Principles of categorization. In *Cognition and categorization*, E. Rosch and R. B. Lloyd (eds). Hillsdale, NJ: Erlbaum.

Rosch, E., C. Simpson and R. S. Miller 1976. Structural bases of typicality effects. *Journal of Experimental Psychology: Human Perception and Performance* 2, 491–502.

Rowe, R. D. and G. Chestnut (eds) 1982. *Managing air quality and scenic quality resources at national parks and wilderness areas*. Boulder, Co: Westview Press.

Slovic, P., D. Fleissner and W. S. Bauman 1972. Analyzing the use of information in investment decision-making: A methodological proposal. *Journal of Business* 45, 283–301.

Slovic, P., L. G. Rorer and P. J. Hoffman, 1971. Analyzing the use of diagnostic signs. *Investigative Radiology* 6, 18–26.

Tversky, B. and K. Hemenway 1983. Categories of environmental scenes. *Cognitive Psychology* 15, 121–49.

Ward, L. M., and J. A. Russell 1981. The psychological representation of molar physical environments. *Journal of Experimental Psychology: General* 110, 121–52.

Wiggins, J. S. 1973. *Personality and prediction: principles of personality assessment*. Reading, Mass.: Addison-Wesley.

Wilson, N. A. B. 1948. The work of the Civil Service Selection Board. *Occupational Psychology* 22, 204–12.

Wohlwill, J. G. 1979. What belongs where: Research on fittingness of man-made structures in natural settings. In *Assessing amenity resource*

values, T. C. Daniel, E. H. Zube and B. L. Driver (eds), 48–57. Fort
Collins, Co: US Forest Service.
Wohlwill, J. F. 1983. The concept of nature: A psychologist's view. In
Human behavior and environment, I. Altman and J. F. Wohlwill (eds),
Vol. 6, 5–37. New York: Plenum Press.
Zube, E. H., J. L. Sell, and J. G. Taylor 1982. Landscape perception:
Research, application and theory. *Landscape Planning* **9**, 1–33.

Critiques and queries

The criticisms and queries listed below are principally just that:
the critical comment, reproduced here to show the divergence of
views amongst those in different corners of the field of landscape
analysis.

John Gittings Perhaps because I was initially trained as a
sociologist/geographer this contribution really appealed. The
interplay between the observer, on the one hand, and the land
form and land use on the other is critical. It sparks off one of my
main interests – the importance of 'the spirit of place', 'the sense of
place' and the interrelationship between 'time, space and movement in landscape', a theme so beautifully examined by Dame
Freya Stark in many of her writings.

Muriel Laverack I could not penetrate the language barrier,
although Fig. 4.1 suggests that had I been able to do so, common
ground might have been reached.

Stephen Daniels Craik unintentionally raises the equation of
language and knowledge. What is the better language for
conceptualising and articulating issues of meaning and value in
landscape? Goodey's popspeak? Craik's technospeak? In Craik's
paper we read the rhetoric (litany?) of systems analysis. Society is
described in terms of 'structures', 'regulatory principles', 'capacities', 'adjustment mechanisms' etc. And so is everything else.
Surely we are no longer innocent of the ideological implications
of this language or its intellectual bankruptcy.

Denis Cosgrove I do not find the focus of this chapter on
individual views of landscape particularly rewarding or relevant
because I regard landscape primarily as a social construct. The
idea of two worldviews, liberal and conservative, points towards
a more important set of ideas but unless the social origins of

these views are specified more precisely and their implications explored, they do not take us very far and are weak analytic concepts. Rather than the 'general relations between political orientation and landscape meanings and values' (p. 55), I would want to study them in historical specificity. Self-expression of status in the landscape is an important issue and a great deal of study is being undertaken on it. This will of necessity be cross-disciplinary.

5 *The vernacular landscape*

J. B. JACKSON

The nature of the landscape, and our way of perceiving it, are the topics which bring this volume together. My own approach lacks the aesthetic and psychological ingredients which give the other chapters their value; I have been chiefly concerned with the commonplace question of what the word means in everyday usage, and especially with its meaning in our north-west European and North American history.

The meanings of 'landscape'

Landscape is a compound word, and its components hark back to that ancient Indo-European idiom, brought out of Asia by migrating peoples thousands of years ago, that became the basis of almost all modern European languages: Latin or Celtic or Germanic or Slavic or Greek. The word was undoubtedly introduced into Britain some time after the 5th century AD by the Angles and Saxons and Jutes and Danes, and other groups of Germanic speech.

In addition to its Old English variations – 'landskipe', 'land-scaef' and others – there is the German *'landschaft'*, the Dutch *'landscap'*, as well as Danish and Swedish equivalents. They all come from the same roots, but they are not always used in the English sense. A German *'landschaft'* can sometimes be a small administrative unit. I have the feeling that there is evolving a slight but noticeable difference between the way Americans use the word and the way the English do. Americans tend to think that landscape can mean natural scenery, whereas in England a landscape almost always contains a human element.

As for the equivalent word in Latin languages, it derives in almost every case from the Latin *'pagus'* meaning a defined rural district. The French have several words for landscape, each with shades of meaning: *'terroir'*, *'pays'*, *'paysage'*, *'campagne'*. In England the distinction was once made between two kinds of landscape: woodland and champion, the latter deriving from the Old French *champagne*, meaning a countryside of fields.

That first syllable, 'land', has had a varied career. By the time it reached England it had acquired a broad meaning. It signified 'earth' and 'soil' as well as a portion of the surface of the globe. But a much earlier Gothic meaning was 'ploughed field'. Grimm's monumental dictionary of the German language says that 'land originally signified the plot of ground or the furrows in a field that were annually rotated' or redistributed. We can assume that in the Dark Ages the most common use of the word indicated any well defined portion of the earth's surface. A small farm plot was a land, and so was a sovereign territory like England or Scotland; any area with recognised boundaries was a land. It is worth noting that despite almost two thousand years of re-interpretation by geographers, poets and ecologists, 'land' in American and English law remains stubbornly true to that ancient meaning: 'any *definite* site (emphasis added) regarded as a portion of the earth's surface, and extending in both vertical directions as defined by law'.

That perhaps is why farmers think of land not only in terms of soil and topography but in terms of spatial measurements, as a defined portion of a wider area. In the American South, and in England too, a 'land' is a subdivision of a field, a broad row made by ploughing or mowing, and horsedrawn mowers were once advertised as 'making a land of so-and-so many feet'. In Yorkshire the reapers of wheat take a 'land' (generally six feet wide) and go down the length of the field. 'A woman' (says the *English Dialect Dictionary*) 'would thus reap half an acre a day and a man an acre'. The *Oxford Dictionary* tells us that a land is 'one of the strips into which a cornfield . . . is divided by water-furrows. (The word) is often taken as a measure of land area and of length, of value varying according to local custom'; and in his book on English field systems, Gray (1915) mentions a typical medieval village where the two large open fields 'consisted of about two thousand long narrow "lands" or selions (furrows) each containing usually from one fourth of an acre to an acre'.

All this is confusing, and even more confusing is the fact that to this day in Scotland a 'land' means a building divided into 'houses' or flats. This particular use of the word is hard to decipher, except that in Gaelic the word '*lann*' means an enclosed space. Finally, here is an example – if it can be called that – of 'land' meaning both a fraction of a larger space and an enclosed space; infantrymen know that a 'land' is an interval between the grooves of a rifle bore.

Thus, as far back as we can trace the word, 'land' meant a defined space, a space with boundaries, though not necessarily one with fences or walls. It is a word with so many derivative meanings that it rivals in ambiguity the word landscape itself. Three centuries ago it was still being used in everyday speech to signify a fraction of ploughed ground no larger than a quarter acre, also to signify an expanse of village holdings, as in grassland or woodland, and also finally to signify England itself – the largest space any Englishman of those days could imagine; in short, a word always implying a space defined by people, something that could be described in objective terms.

This brings us to that second syllable: 'scape'. It is essentially the same as 'shape', except that it once meant a composition of *similar* objects, as when we speak of a fellowship or a membership. The meaning is clearer in a related word: 'sheaf' – a bundle or collection of similar stalks or plants. Old English or Anglo-Saxon seems to have contained several compound words using the second syllable – 'scape' or its equivalent – to indicate collective aspects of the environment. It is much as if the words had been coined when people began to see the complexities of the man-made world. Thus 'housescape' meant what we would now call a household, and a word of the same sort which we still use – 'township' – once meant a collection of 'tuns' or farmsteads.

Taken apart in this manner 'landscape' appears to be an easily understood word: a collection of lands. But both syllables once had several distinct, now forgotten, meanings and this should alert us to the fact that familiar monosyllables in England – house, town, land, field, home, etc. – can be very shifty despite their countrified sound. 'Scape' is an instance. An English document of the tenth century mentions the destruction of what it called a 'waterscape'. What could that have been? We might logically suppose that it was the liquid equivalent of a landscape, an ornamental arrangement, perhaps, of ponds and brooks and waterfalls. But it was actually something different. The waterscape in question was a system of pipes and drains and aqueducts serving a residence and a mill.

From this piece of information we can learn two things: first, that our Dark Age forebears possessed skills which we seldom credit them with, and, secondly, that the word 'scape' could also indicate something like an organisation or a system. If 'housescape' meant the organisation of the personnel of a house, if 'township' eventually came to mean an administrative unit, then 'landscape' could well have meant something like an organisation, a system of rural farm spaces. At all events it is clear to me that a thousand years ago the word had nothing to do with scenery or the depiction of scenery.

Nevertheless that formula: landscape as a composition of man-made spaces on the land, is more significant than it first appears, for if it does not provide us with a definition it throws a revealing light on the origin of the concept. For it says that a landscape is not a natural feature of the environment but a *synthetic* space, a man-made system functioning and evolving not according to natural laws but to serve a community – for the collective character of the landscape is one thing that all generations and all points of view have agreed upon. A landscape is thus a space deliberately created to speed up or slow down the process of nature. As Eliade expresses it, it represents man taking upon himself the role of time.

We are probably safe in assuming that in the Anglo-Saxon countryside the word 'land' was primarily used to describe a patch of cultivated ground – the most valuable kind – and that a landscape was essentially a system of such spaces, the fields and plots used by the inhabitants of the village for raising crops. It must have been a word much used by villagers and peasants and farmhands, but little used by others. For the fact is 'landscape' rarely if ever occurs in legal documents. The Domesday Book, a remarkable inventory of landholdings compiled by order of William the Conqueror in the 11th century was, to be sure, written in Latin, but no translation ever mentioned 'landscape' and indeed the word seems to have gradually fallen into disuse.

Two centuries after the Conquest a brand new term, imported from France although of Latin origin, took its place. It derived from *contra*, against or opposite: that which lies opposite or confronting the viewer, the landscape spread out before one. Originally it seems to have indicated a tract of land of undefined extent, a region, but by the 14th century it came to mean (according to the *Oxford English Dictionary*) a district having more or less definite limits in relation to human occupation: owned, that is to say, by the same lord or proprietor, or inhabited by people of the same race, dialect, occupation, all having customs and traditions of their own and benefiting from certain local rights and privileges. Countryside seems to be a Scottish variant on country, and it likewise suggests a tract of country having a kind of natural or human unity.

Both these words, 'landscape' and 'country', have at least one thing in common: they indicate a tract of land which can be seen at a glance, which can be identified as a unit, a territory, usually the territory of a small rural community. Both words have of course

acquired new and broader meanings. But I believe I am right in
suspecting that neither of them had any legal standing; that both
were associated with the peasantry, and suggested the territory of
an impoverished and illiterate population with no written history,
no written laws or records, and no documented title to the land it
occupied.

'Political' and 'vernacular' landscapes

In the perception of the crown, the nobility, and the clergy such
peasant territories had little importance; clusters of small, temporary, crudely measured spaces which constantly changed hands
and even changed in shape and size and use. The land which these
fortunate persons possessed – the estate of the noblemen, or of a
bishop, the forest of the king, to say nothing of his kingdom – all
had a definite, almost sacred origin, with sacrosanct boundaries
vouched for in a treaty or charter. Moreover they served an entirely different purpose: not year-by-year survival, but economic
and political power: the power to collect taxes, administer law,
raise armies and accumulate wealth.

That is where we can draw one distinction between what I call
the vernacular landscape – that of the village or rural community –
and the aristocratic or political landscape of the crown and the
nobility: the vernacular landscape seeks to include a small (and
visible) territory essential to its survival and to its kind of
agriculture, whereas the political landscape largely ignores
topography in favour of strategic or economic strong points. In
his *Economic and social history of the Middle Ages*, J. W. Thompson
(1959) describes the way in which the Empire of Charlemagne
was divided among his heirs:

> A form of partition in which bishoprics, abbeys, counties, and crown
> lands were dealt out like a pack of cards, ignoring and violating any
> distinction of natural boundary or of race or of language which might
> inconvenience an even economic settlement. The frontiers between
> kingdoms formed a confused and intricate network sometimes
> coinciding, sometimes not, with differences of race and language,
> sometimes following for a few miles a natural line of division like a
> river, but as often as not crossing rivers and leaping ranges . . . There
> was no sense of either social or territorial amplitude, no sentiment
> either of nation or of country.

According to Peter Hunter Blair, the same arbitrary non-
geographical boundary prevailed in Anglo-Saxon England
between the various kingdoms and even between the shires.

Insofar as that medieval political or aristocratic landscape was the creation of legal decisions, long range policies, and competition for power and land and subjects, it can be studied like a map, with definite boundaries and monuments and highways, and a visible, relatively permanent spatial organization. It can be read as a chapter in history, or studied as an illustration of political change.

But the vernacular medieval landscape – or its many component examples – is more elusive. Its history is, in the current phrase, a history without events – or at least without recorded events – and we see it as the slow procession of generations of farmers and stockmen and foresters and hunters and migrants, leaving few traces behind of the expansion of fields and villages, the coming of small settlements, their gradual growth and sometimes their disappearance. What survives is less a matter of ruins and half obliterated boundaries than of legends.

How are we to begin to understand what we now conveniently call the perception of the landscape among these centuries of anonymous and inarticulate people? All that we can turn to, aside from the invaluable work of archeologists and rural historians, are the unwritten, all but mythical evidences of the past. These are still part of our everyday – one might almost say our domestic – heritage: fairy tales, figures of speech, superstitions and customs and ways of working and celebrating. We even run across reminders of our vernacular past in local laws and ordinances inherited intact from earlier generations and from other parts of the Western world. It is, of course, no easy task to use this material in the reconstruction of an ancient landscape, and we are likely to lose our way in the confusion of legend and poetry and fiction.

All that we can hope to glimpse is how a rural and predominantly illiterate peasant population envisioned the organisation of their local spaces and how it saw its role in the functioning and preservation of that landscape. There is one source for insight into that perception in the works of Jacob Grimm: not so much his mythology or collection of fairy tales or his dictionary, but his *Deutsche Rechtsaltertümer* – Germanic Legal Antiquities (1828). Published more than 150 years ago, it is an immense multilingual compilation of local laws and customs from all over northwestern Europe that relate to property, rank, social relationships, and the administration of customary law. In many cases the material dates back to the 5th century AD; in others the material is still alive, so to speak, as of 1825. The laws and customs were collected from early Germanic codes, from poems and sagas and from local legal records. One way of proceeding through this two-volume mass of obscure information is to look for indications or hints as to how landscapes or settlements were originally formed, whether in western Germany, Scandinavia, Britain or Iceland.

There are, as we might expect, plenty of references to newly established settlements or colonies, and as we might also expect, there is a leader, a military leader or the head of a family, who, with his followers, descends on some presumably empty or deserted territory and claims it as his own. Some omen, some apparition, some sign has identified the place he and his followers are to occupy. How does he (or they) establish the extent of the land they want? In a chapter entitled 'Measurement', Grimm suggests that every legal decision made by the ancient Germanic peoples was always influenced by some ominous or mysterious factor: the appearance of a flight of birds, or an unforeseen gesture, and that the location of boundaries, a very solemn event, always involved some unforeseen hazard or interpretation: it might be a question of how far a hen could fly, or how many miles a man could ride before the king awoke from his sleep. According to Geoffrey of Monmouth, when Hengist arrived in Britain he asked for the amount of land which could be covered by the hide of an ox; when this was granted he slit a hide into innumerable thin strips, and thereby enclosed a sizeable piece of land. The practice seems to have been popular in Anglo-Saxon England. One might suppose that in the course of time it would have been seen through; but an early trickster by the name of Ivar managed to stretch the strips of his ox hide to such an extent that he gained possession of a large piece of real estate, where he built a city called Lundonaborg.

Land and ownership

However acquired, and however extensive, the newly settled land became the property of the leader. He allotted portions of it to his followers, and his sons (and their heirs) received pieces of land outright yet (according to this vernacular interpretation of landscape history) no natural elements in the landscape could be owned or controlled by an individual. That is to say no one without general consent could control and exploit fire, water, earth, or air.

If this seems obvious, we should bear in mind that the building of a masonry bridge in the early Middle Ages was considered a dangerous and almost sacrilegious undertaking, and that the building of a dam or of a water mill was a matter of public concern. Seventeenth-century New England placed special restrictions and controls on every miller using water, and although the reasons are now strictly economic or ecological we control the use of flowing water in America as rigidly as it was controlled in Medieval Europe. Fire was likewise seen as community property, perhaps deriving from the hearth of the ancestral homestead; in any case a severe form of punishment in a village was deprivation of fire and water – the fire presumably coming from a neighbour at a time when kindling a fire was no easy task. As for public control of air, I find it hard to imagine what this could have meant; except that air was possibly interpreted as wind. For it was a general rule that branches and fruit brought down by the wind were common property. The earth as a common good was a more complicated concept, for it seems to have meant that the earth – or the surface of the earth – in its natural state could not be individual property. The earth in its natural state was undoubtedly far more extensive a thousand years ago than it is now. It then included the forest, the meadow land (with its stands of natural grass) and even the field; indeed in Medieval England the word did not mean a cultivated, well defined, man-made space, it meant 'land free from wood, lying on downs and moors, or sometimes in the open spaces of the forest'.

The meadow, the forest, and the field were therefore aspects of the natural environment that no one could own, and according to Grimm in none of those spaces was a permanent fence or hedge ever allowed, though the space itself might well be bounded and protected. This absence of permanent fences is what we mean of course when we refer to the open field system; it also characterised the meadow which was shared by all villagers; and though there were temporary fences in the forest, anyone who sought to enclose permanently and appropriate a portion of the forest was severely punished: his oven (the element of fire, I suppose) was destroyed, and his well was filled in. There even seems to have been a persistent effort to enlarge these natural spaces in the landscape. Again, according to Grimm, if a field was neglected and abandoned so that even one tree grew on it, it automatically became community forest. Part of the fascination of Grimm's compilation is the various ways in which village authorities all over northwestern Europe determined whether an abandoned field had reverted: the tree should provide shade to a sleeping cow; it should reach to the shoulder of a man on horseback; it should be large enough to impede ploughing, and so on.

This extensive area of natural spaces – forest and field and meadow and moor – served the needs of the stockman, the herder, the shepherd, all of whom used land which was undivided and where animals could be grazed under community control. But as farming grew in importance there inevitably evolved within each landscape a number of spaces privately controlled and surrounded with fence or hedge; two ways of organising space, and two ways of defining it. The older pastoral tradition conceived of wealth in terms of livestock: movable, negotiable, capable of being held, and of increasing in value over time, and not identified with any particular place: cattle or chattel or (to use the modern form of the word) capital; movable property which the individual could accumulate or dispose of as he saw fit. The other kind of wealth was land: something the family held on to and bequeathed, if possible, to the next generation, intact and as serviceable as ever: a visible, well defined, permanent sign of membership in the community.

The distinction between the two is of course very ancient, and poetry and legend, particularly in northwestern Europe, have romanticised the herders' way of life: he was the horseman, free to wander and seek adventure, moving his livestock from the valley into the hills and mountains according to the season, far from fences and ploughed fields and villages. Nevertheless, in the course of time the farmer took over more and more of the village land and the herder was gradually pushed into the forest and wasteland; the distinction was no longer seen as one between two ways of life, but as one between the landholder and the landless, between those who possessed immobile wealth and those whose only wealth was movable.

Generally speaking movable property was the only possession of women, minors, and those of the lowest status, but the concept was very flexible, and there are instances when the correct term would seem to have been something like transient or temporary or destined to perish: anything which can be carried away and consumed. The French word '*denrée*', meaning both commodities and money, is suggestive. In the vernacular landscape we are exploring, movable property included not only livestock but household goods, weapons, bees, and even certain vegetable products. Thus in certain regions mobile property meant grass (and crops) moved by the wind. The peasant who leased or was granted land could use only the surface – nine inches, I believe, was the depth to which they could plough – to raise a movable crop or graze his movable livestock. But each village had its own interpretation; in some places hedges, fences, and implements were considered movable, and it was almost universal to consider the wooden houses or cottages of mud and brush and thatch, without a foundation, as movable goods.

Nor was this simply a convenient legal fiction allowing the house to be sold independent of the land or bequeathed to the widow or daughter instead of to the son who automatically inherited the family dwelling. The definition did much in fact to determine the construction of the cottage or small peasant house: thus it was deliberately built in a flimsy and inexpensive manner so that if the landlord demanded its removal or if a job was available somewhere else the family could disassemble the dwelling and reassemble it in another location. Braudel mentions the relative mobility of villages and hamlets in the latter Middle Ages:

> They grew up, expanded, contracted, and also shifted their sites. Sometimes these 'desertions' were total and final . . . More often the centre of gravity within a given cultural area shifted, and everything – furniture, people, animals, stones – was moved out of the abandoned village to a site a few kilometers away. Even the form of the village could change in the course of these vicissitudes.

Mobility of a less dramatic sort characterised the shape and size of the individual parcels in the open fields of the village. Divisions brought about by inheritance, consolidations and sales, and gradual shifts in boundaries when a neighbour surreptitiously ploughed one more furrow along the line, all of these after a few generations produced such a distortion and confusion that drastic re-organisation and re-ordering was called for. There were economic and technological reasons for this shifting of boundaries, which was not confined to the open fields. Even many of the country roads or lanes – the roads to work and the roads from pasture to village – were essentially rights of way, closed or abandoned after their usefulness was over.

Spaces in the vernacular landscape

In the end, all we can say about the vernacular landscape, wherever it is to be found, is that its spaces are subject to frequent and unpredictable changes in use, in ownership and in dimensions. That there is always an immense amount of common or collective spaces where natural resources are exploited by individuals in a piecemeal manner to satisfy their own domestic needs, and that there long survives the belief in natural or aboriginal spaces, which like the four basic elements belong to the local population and are therefore never to be used exclusively for private profit.

The right to use these resources derives not from any conviction that mankind is part of a natural order, and therefore justified in exploiting the land, but from membership in a family- or leader-centred community: a web of interpersonal relationships produces and preserves the vernacular landscape, not a direct relationship with the environment itself. What we see around us symbolises the mysterious, semi-divine landscape which that legendary, semi-divine ancestor chose for us, countless centuries ago; and that is why its basic spaces, its basic composition must be preserved.

A recent writer on the English village (Muir 1980) suggests that the Saxon founders of a landscape 'chose their site carefully, looking for a spot that would furnish them with all the resources necessary for a tolerable and self sufficient life . . . access to a reliable source of fresh water . . . Then, in declining order of attraction . . . access to ploughland, meadow grazing land, fuel and building materials, and a flattish well-drained site' for the village.

There were thus three essential spaces: village, arable, and grazing – for the forest was primarily valued for its grass and lawns, the glens and clearings where livestock could feed. The most extensive of the three, at least in the earlier centuries, would have been the one devoted to grazing: forest and pasture. Yet as Duby remarks in his history of the Medieval landscape,

> arable and grazing, *ager* and *saltus*, *Allmende* and *Gewannen* . . ., the combination seems in effect to be constant and fundamental throughout the Middle Ages: three concentric zones, so to speak, the village enclosure, the cultivated fields devoted to grain, and finally a wide belt of uncultivated land: such was the image which [a writer of the 12th century] retained of the village of his childhood: three zones where the human presence, the works of men, gradually diminish as we move out from the centre, but three zones all equally useful, equally productive.

The ideal vernacular landscape was thus a series of three concentric spaces. In reality, of course, they were *not* concentric, but in the Medieval mind this was how the cosmos was organised: the Almighty in the centre, then the heavens, then the earth. We have almost forgotten how devoted we once were, in our remote past, to the number three. There were three celestial spheres, three classes in society, three spaces in the landscape, three fields. Once there were three seasons instead of four. The calendar, even then, contained many three-day holidays; the laws of Wales

were written as triads. Fairy tales tell us of three wishes, three
sons, three guesses. In one form or another we repeat the German
saying that all good things come in threes.

Nothing has been more characteristic of our traditional northwestern European/Anglo-American landscape than the persist-
ence of this triad of spaces; woodland and grazing, pasture, and
fields together, though in a variety of forms and relationships,
they comprised all the lasting and rewarding elements in a rural
way of life.

Thus in the 17th century, when Englishmen arrived in New
England, they organised their towns or villages in strict accord-
ance with the old Medieval system. Each qualified inhabitant of a
new settlement was granted, in addition to a homelot in the
village itself, a portion of meadow, a portion of land for tillage,
and a woodlot of generous size. And though the prompt decay of
the traditional open field system and the development of private
farms independently operated put an end to the search for village
self-sufficiency, the belief that every farm should automatically
contain meadow, field, and woodland remained as strong as ever.
The New England farmer or Georgical dictionary, compiled in 1797,
recommended that 'lots designed chiefly for tillage should be
nearest to the house and barn . . . The mowing lots for pasturage
should be contrived to be next, and the woodlots furthest of all
lots from the house'. The reason offered for each location was
convenience and the saving of labour. Even so, the Medieval
hierarchy of spaces, the system of three concentric zones, was still
discernible.

By the beginning of the 20th century the almost total re-
organisation of the American farm, its increasing mechanisation,
its emphasis on one commercial crop, and the declining usefulness of the woodlot, opened the eyes of most farmers to the
impracticability of the three-part division of the landscape. We
have now devised entirely new ways of defining land, based
partly on soil analysis, partly on terrain – an indication, I think,
that we have gone a long way toward formulating a new
definition of landscape itself.

References

Braudel, F. 1981. *Civilisation and capitalism* (3 vols). London: Collins.
Duby, G. 1968. *Rural economy and country life in the medieval West*.
    Columbia, S. Carolina: University of South Carolina Press.
Gray, H. L. 1915. *English field systems*. Cambridge, Mass.: Harvard
    University Press.

Muir, R. 1980. *The English village*. London: Thames and Hudson.
Thompson, J. W. 1959. *Economic and social history of the Middle Ages*. New York: Ungar.

Critiques and queries

The discussion points below are selected to highlight divergencies from Brinck Jackson's perspective. They complement the many commendations of his delightful writing which are not included here.

Denis Cosgrove As always, Brinck Jackson is a pleasure to read and much of what he says prompts both the critical intellect and the imagination. I am sent musing into the world of the Anglo-Saxon villager, seeing in reverie the world from his eyes.

But in its strength is also the weakness of this analysis. While it weaves a delightful dance through the etymological forest of landscape, land, country and other topographical words, it is unclear precisely where it is headed or what we are really seeking. Points of considerable significance suddenly appear but pass by. Some of the assumptions are very large and somewhat unfounded, for example that because 'landscape' does not occur in Medieval documents it referred to the territory of 'an impoverished and illiterate population with no written history' (p. 69). Jackson's populist view of landscape is a healthy antidote to the normal focus on elite landscape but it can be pressed too far.

Dick Watson Jackson writes about the land as England itself (p. 67): this is often emotionally charged, in a way that Jackson neglects: see John of Gaunt's speech in *Richard II*, II.i ('The royal throne of kings' etc):

> This land of such dear souls, this dear dear land . . .

This point leads me into another. Why are we likely to 'lose our way in the confusion of legend and poetry and fiction'? I see this as a fundamental point, perhaps the most important one I have to make: we cannot treat landscape as something measurable and capable of investigation through changes of word-meaning (as this interesting chapter does). We *have* to include imaginative writing, because the most important perceptive tool which we bring with us in the contemplation of landscape is the *imagination*.

All the poets and novelists do this instinctively, and we can learn from them, just as we can learn from historians about how the landscape came to be in its present state. Jackson's analysis turns its back on the imagination, and there is a tendency in landscape studies to do the same (principally because it seems unscientific). I am against this tendency: I affirm the importance of imaginative feeling in the human approach to landscape, and the complex interaction of subjective and objective in the perception of the external world.

Ian Brotherton   I found this paper fascinating though tantalising. Fascinating, because it probes the meaning of the word landscape, which must be fundamental, and because it contains useful insights into the characteristics of vernacular landscape. It is tantalising because the contrasts that need to be drawn are barely touched. How, for example, do the original meanings of the word landscape relate to modern meanings. What do the changes in meaning signify? And what distinguishes, in cultural, social and physical terms, the vernacular landscape from aristocratic, the technocratic, the bureaucratic and all the other '-atic' and '-istic' landscape types?

Muriel Laverack   I find it unprofitable to distinguish, as Jackson does, too sharply between vernacular and political landscapes. Power structures throughout the ages have determined how land has been used and organised, and the more politicised and power structured the society, the more the land has reflected it: division, defence, exploitation, investment, productivity, technology. I cannot agree that the procession of men and their land-uses through many generations has left little but legends. 'Envisioning' how the country space was organised is not the only insight: in England we *know* a lot, historically, and can still see much of the palimpsest on the ground (though I agree it is being destroyed at a faster rate since 1945 than before).

Stephen Daniels   Jackson has proposed an eccentric definition of landscape, one that contrasts with and actively questions most modern uses of the term. Specifically he has stripped away its aesthetic varnish to reveal the grain of everyday life on and with the land. This is fine; Jackson has been doing this with concrete examples for years now, reformulating landscape as essentially something that people live in not just look at. But if there is a historical pedigree for this definition the one Jackson has presented in this essay seems not to be it. His strategy is intriguing. He makes an analytical separation of the word into 'land' and 'scape' and maintains that these two terms separately

(a)

Plate 2.1 Some African savanna trees: (a) *Acacia tortilis*, a species characteristic of moist areas where subsurface water can be tapped by deep rooted trees; (b) *Acacia recifiens*, a species of dry savannas.

(b)

(a)

Plate 2.2 Dominant trees of Japanese gardens: (a) *Acer palmatum*; (b) *Pinus densiflora*.

(b)

Plate 2.3 Formal European gardens: (a) Villa La Gamberaia, Florence, Italy.

Plate 2.3 *(continued)*: (b) Vaux le Vicomte, France.

have the unsophisticated connotations that he appreciates; then he
conjoins these terms into 'landscape' maintaining that this merely
adds the meanings of the two terms as 'collection of lands'. But it
did not happen this way in history. The historical joining
transformed the meaning of the two terms and what emerged was a
sophisticated new meaning at least in English with connotations of
separation from the possession of land and perception mediated
by various devices such as mirrors and perspective.

John Gittins   For many of us engaged in landscape, be it as
designers, planners, managers, researchers, artists, writers or
poets, J. B. Jackson is a colourful and seminal figure. His journal,
Landscape, is a major platform for the communication of ideas and
opinions. The chapter, however, tends towards a discursive,
rambling semantic compilation of facts and interpretations. Only
if the term 'vernacular' is taken to mean the commonplace do we
get some historical perspectives.

On points of detail I am not convinced, for example, that
landscape is 'a space deliberately created to speed up or slow down
the process of Nature'. For me, the discussion of 'space' lacks
precision, for space like place is at the very basis of our theme of
landscape meanings and values. Neither do I subscribe to his view
that 'what survives of the Medieval landscape is less a matter of
ruins and half obliterated boundaries than of legends'. As I walk
across known landscapes and consult those landscape re-
positories, the Ordnance Survey sheets, my eyes tell me that this
is not so.

Brinck Jackson replies: The comments on my paper have in
every case given me much to think about. They have made me
wish that I could rephrase many passages and eliminate others,
if only better to explain my thesis. But it would be briefer if I
merely said that the paper was in fact a fragment, an incomplete
argument for a re-definition of the word 'landscape' that would
combine the aesthetic with the historical approach.

I was mistaken in assuming that everyone was aware that
the current usage of the word landscape derives not from the
Anglo-Saxon or Medieval English (which, as I suggested, went
out of circulation many centuries ago) but from the Dutch word
'*landscap*' introduced in the late 16th century to England by art
dealers and art critics who translated it as meaning 'a picture of
(Dutch) inland scenery'. Thereafter it remained identified with an
aesthetic experience, either of a kind of painting or of rural
scenery.

It was certainly no coincidence that this new awareness of the aesthetic nature of landscape emerged at a period when a new kind of topographical writing flourished throughout the Western world, and especially in England. Beginning with Harrison's *Description of Britain* in 1577 and carried on by Evelyn, Celia Fiennes, Defoe, Arthur Young, Cobbett, and even by Samuel Johnson, a remarkable series of landscape descriptions appeared, giving vivid glimpses of the changes taking place throughout English towns and countrysides. But none of these was the work of students of the landscape as art: they were written by geographers and travellers, agricultural experts or social commentators. Very few of these works are now referred to in the literature of landscape description. Though they were valuable accounts of landscape history they have been neglected in favour of the discussion of Kent and Capability Brown, and Chambers and Gilpin. The Romantic Movement further emphasised the estrangement between the study of the cultural landscape and the 'natural' landscape, with the result that in the United States at least landscape is now defined by many writers on environmental matters as that part of our environment that has not been modified by the presence of man – preferably wilderness.

I confess that I find the more extreme – and more vocal – forms of American environmentalism to be irresponsible and uncivilised. The best solution I see for this super-aestheticism is a more general recognition of landscape history: less emphasis on the old romantic theme of conflict between man and nature and more emphasis on the political, economic and technological forces which continue to shape our landscapes. I find it encouraging that several American universities now offer courses on the history of our cultural landscape in which such mundane topics as roads and settlement patterns and sports facilities and gardens are discussed, and their evolution touched upon. Contrary to what many might suppose, this kind of education does not foster a purely sociological, objective understanding; on the contrary it has often fostered a genuine affection and sense of responsibility for the small-scale local landscape and its development.

Ian Brotherton quite rightly suggests that the notion of the vernacular landscape calls for further definition. I am aware of the dangers of dwelling too much on the commonplace everyday aspects of our surroundings; and it is essential that the more permanent, more formal, *designed* features be included. If I may quote from my book on the vernacular landscape:

A (vernacular) landscape without visible signs of political history is a landscape without memory or forethought. We are inclined in America to think that the value of monuments is simply to remind us of origins. They are much more valuable as reminders of long-range collective purpose, of goals and objectives and principles. As such even the least sightly of monuments gives a landscape beauty and dignity and keeps the collective memory alive.

6 Spotting, squatting, sitting or setting: some public images of landscape

BRIAN GOODEY

> Several times a year Anne arranged to take him on short motor tours to see the incredibly various aspects of the landscape in Great Britain. They went to Yorkshire, Derbyshire, to the Lake District, the West Country and Cornwall. When I was able to, I went with them. It fascinated me to watch Edward when the car halted by some especially splendid spread of hills, moorland, and deep valleys. He sat very still and his face appeared completely impassive. He might, I thought, have been staring at a blank wall, until I saw the intensity of his gaze.
>
> I do not remember Edward ever making any sort of note: not even the faintest scribble; yet weeks, even months later, the shape, the tones, those moors, hills, and valleys he had looked at so intently, would appear on paper. I am convinced he possessed a unique mental capacity (wholly denied to most people) to absorb, and *never forget*, any images he truly observed.
>
> William Chappell (1982, p. 112)

I want in this chapter to consider some aspects of the public image of and response to landscape. The task embodies such presumption that the title should serve as a reminder to the author, as well as the reader, that a vast number of images and values are involved. For example, there are those of the spotter, detecting target train, bird, building or manhole cover against the landscape backdrop; and those of the squatter, seeking to become part of a landscape and the values which it may be seen as retaining from past cultures. Then again there are those satisfied with sitting, resting in and consuming views or atmosphere on an occasional basis, and those, rather fewer in number, who may have evident landscape as the setting for their everyday activities.

By mentioning 'evident' landscape we touch on an initial problem which will rumble, like distant thunder, throughout this exploration. Either landscape is everything, everywhere, every view and every place (and therefore indiscernible: nothing, nowhere, no view and non-place) or it is something selected, drawn from context by being framed in space or described in terms which endorse its rarity or raise its value. Whilst it might be more honest to underline the general, these comments light upon the specific in much the same way as any educative activity with a practice goal must isolate particular items for analysis.

On being forced to focus: convergence and discontinuity in student views

The problem of landscape identity has been a 'live' one in my teaching: how can one focus incoming undergraduate minds on matters of environmental quality without imposing any more values than their arrival on a Town Planning course may already have occasioned? In recent years I have attempted to solve this by early, individual, visits to designated areas or urban/suburban Oxford, with two challenges posed:

(a) *'A place where you are at peace with yourself'*. Already words shape expectations and, perhaps, raise emotions which are hardly formed. Most students find some difficulty with 'at peace' and resort to learning rather than experience of place for their response. In discussion the ability to sit and view distance ('vista') with what passes as 'natural' greenspace and possibly some water seems to be a major precondition of 'peace'. Evidence of tradition in built form, the order and recognisable images which come with age, are an added bonus to such a landscape of calm. In short, the Cullenesque view, the preferred 'arcadia' of the Essex Design Guide, seem either to have been appropriate consolidations of English landscape tastes, or to have had more propaganda impact in secondary education than might have been expected.

(b) *'A place where you are frightened'* . . . or at least uncomfortable? Few students will admit to fright. Not quite the reverse of the above, especially as 'place' rather than a 'view' emerges more frequently in the responses. A more difficult question, with fewer available judgements against which to check personal experience. Traffic, noise, bleakness stemming from built-form uniformity (though seldom from uniform 'natural' environments), newness, and a collection of observations which add up to brashness; all these feature in responses to this challenge. A wide range of locations and scales of environment are reflected in replies.

After some ten years of pursuing this introductory task with students, as well as with some teachers and school pupils, I have little doubt that the distant view of green, rolling, wooded hills with clusters of vernacular buildings, indicative of man's rooted, harmonious consort with time and nature, offer the greatest potential for peace and calm (Patience Strong calendars *passim*). In this sense there is an 'English Landscape Taste' which seems culturally transmitted and which is likely to be endorsed by the majority, although the age and class bias of my respondents should be recognised. So too must be the minority report, the inevitable discussion which follows the exercise, in which a number of students quickly point to the restrictive traditional values implicit in such landscape preferences. For there is little place in such perspectives for industry, for evidence of work, or even for people, who seldom if ever inhabit the peaceful scene. A vision of solitude is inevitably encouraged by the form of my question. There is a realisation, too, that the new – though often essential – is usually unacceptable as part of the landscape until a generation has grown up finding the element *in situ*.

For the majority, our subsequent discussions usually portray the landscape as part of heritage, a link with the misty past, an unspoilt world beyond more immediate despoliation, its elements, activities and design all tied closely to a mystery which should be enjoyed without mention of management or change. Landscape shares with the Royal Family, Motherhood and History a sanctity and encapsulated charm which many, perhaps most, people do not wish to penetrate.

On public images

Much of what follows represents an attempt to disaggregate generalisations concerning 'public' and 'landscape' to upset the convenient picture maintained by culture. The reason for doing so is not only the 'Everest response' – 'because it is there' – but also because the warm, cosy image of landscape does not provide an operational base from which to maintain or manage: the charm capsule contains the seed of its own destruction.

'Scapes'

What evidence is there for unravelling 'landscape' in popular language or literature? In Britain, at least, the word implies a predominantly 'green' or 'natural' environment, or a pictorial reproduction of it; it therefore precludes and/or renders negative those urban environments in which most of us live. *Townscape* remains a professional rather than public term but carries with it the positive images ascribed to it by Gordon Cullen (rather than Ian Nairn) as well as the design values of the 'townscape tradition' which, whilst hotly contested in the design studio, have taken strong root in local development control offices. *Greenscape* is an ugly term but does have the advantage of linking rural landscape with urban greenspace as a subject for professional attention. The discipline of *Landscape Architecture* has not always served its subject well and *Landscaping* (a term favoured by tarmacadam drive makers and turf layers) may only have served to diminish the profession in the public eye. (Parenthetically, the Landscape Architecture profession in the USA seems to have been more effective in conveying both the breadth of interests and the applicability of its skills than its counterpart in the United Kingdom.)

There is a dreadful poverty in public landscape descriptors ('what a nice/lovely/breathtaking view') and a few more 'scape' concepts could well be tried. The distinction between 'cultured landscape' and 'wildscape' needs to be fostered and may well meet public favour as man's role in shaping past landscapes is increasingly recognised through television, industrial archaeology or Rural Life Museums. Borrowing back from art, 'seascape' and 'waterscape' are long overdue for more professional, not to say public, airing, as so many resort and recreation attractions rely on the visible interplay between water and land. 'Sunscape' might be a most appropriate reminder of the crucial role which light and weather play in individual appreciation of landscape, whilst the borrowing of 'soundscape' from BBC Radio 3 introductions would provide an apt term for a crucial aspect of place recognition which few are able to identify, but many react to.

Here may be some elements of a useful language for talking about places, but there also has to be the opportunity and desire to develop such a language.

Arcadia revisited

To develop, a language must serve as the medium of exchange for ideas, yet one of the major problems with the language of landscape is that there is no such exchange. Except in minority circles, landscape concepts are part only of information *provision*.

Two current examples are useful. First, the marketing of Essex
Design Guide housing to the individual purchaser, and of plots
and communities to the developer/builder, has been rich in the
terminology of traditional village environments and landscapes:
'native materials', 'fitting', 'detail', 'community', 'age', and
'heritage'. But this is only the language of selling, of appealing to
latent values (or prejudices); it is not a medium of exchange
between the residents of the Essex Design Guide housing areas.
Secondly, the rapid development of 'interpreted' historical and
natural sites has exposed the visitor to a lexicon of terms drawn
from botany, ornithology, industrial archaeology and land
management. Poster displays and booklets offer this novel
terminology but seldom is there an opportunity for on-site verbal
experiment where the elements of the new language could be
absorbed. Possibly the only area in which 'landscape' language is
growing is the individual garden, where a plethora of gardening
books, radio and television programmes endorse other descriptors for man-made mini-environments. The 'ha-ha' is recognised, the 'visual stop' repeated at the top of the garden.

The media has a lot to answer for

Even without the persuasive background commentary of John
Berger and Susan Sontag, it is evident that the media do have
much to answer for when it comes to public interpretation of
landscape. Let us look briefly at three caricatures of media
presentation.

First, 'landscape for passing the port by'. As with building
preservation, the fine arts, classical music and *the* novel (rather
than *a* novel), there have always been those rich enough in time or
financial terms to consider and create taste in landscape. In the
past, experiencing and exploring place was, for some, almost
secondary to collecting place through topographical writings,
watercolours and prints, then photographs, National Geographical film footage, evocative music and, of course, artefacts
which reproduced or reflected place and landscape.

Although this originally was – and continues as – an upper- and
upper-middle class activity, mass production since the Victorian
era has permitted wider participation, and the joy of passing the
port over topographical discussion now extends to passing the
cheeseboard in front of slides or home videos of last summer's
holiday. In both activities language develops around the image
captured by the medium rather than around the landscape
portrayed. Events and detail may be reported, but it is as if the

original landscape is too large or too precious for detailed discussion.

Secondly, 'Pre-Fifties pop'. In the 1930s a tendency developed for popular landscape illustration which deserves note, especially in 1984, the year of Orwell. Its more deliberate statement was in the photographic juxtapositions by Bill Brandt, reflecting high life and poverty in London. But a deliberate attempt to portray, through traditional and new media, the previously unconsidered landscape of Britain was also reflected by painters, poets and composers. Influences and images were legion: Ellington's *Harlem Air Shaft*, Soviet socialist-realist painters and poets, the German architectural 'modern movement', suburban home ownership, the car, and Surrealist painting. As the 1979 London 'Thirties' exhibition showed most forcefully, however, it was the new media, and especially the mass-circulation illustrated paper and the moving picture, which provided the most creative and readily accessible landscape images of the period.

Thirdly, 'And now'. Black-and-white news photography and the cinema documentary have left a strong mark on the way we view landscape and the role we allocate it in our lives. While the moving images are now in full colour and in our homes, and the Brandt black-and-white has been replaced by the coffee table colour, the late 'Thirties' shaped many of our decision-makers and also the patterns of media productions which persist. People made up the active foreground of news photographs and the focus of film, far from being unsightly blots on the calm scene; machines with motion and light captured the attention. Landscape became the backdrop or foil to action, the past 'out there', people and machines were the 'here and now'. The development of this dichotomy may be seen in the pages of *Picture Post* and *Lilliput*; it merges, in literature and art, with the city versus country debate which Williams (1975) and others have traced.

By the time postwar welfare state philosophies were codified on the statute books, landscape was seen as sufficiently apart from daily life, dialogue and concerns to merit special concern, both in terms of public 'amenity' and in the reservations designated as National Parks.

Popular landscape images

I contend, therefore, that landscape must be treated as something apart from daily life. The 'Thirties' and the Welfare State succeeded in severing the public from landscape concerns as a price for saving what was professionally interpreted as being the essence of British landscape heritage. In my view it was a price worth paying. The last years have seen extensive individual and corporate efforts to re-establish links with the world that was saved but lost.

Prints and reproductions

Given that the majority cannot live with a view worthy of the real estate image of landscape seen from the window, there are three immediate paths to a landscape relationship. The first, tripping or visiting, is discussed below. The second, joining an organisation such as the National Trust, which claims both a responsibility and a shared ownership, is a path taken by an increasing number. But the most common path to a relationship is expressed by placing a landscape image on the wall. An honourable tradition, certainly, and with forces at work similar to those that shaped the decorated interior of 150 years ago.

Artists such as Constable, Turner, Cotman and Cox were well aware of the interplay between creativity and public taste, and both the 'original' artist and the print or reproduction maker of today seem to follow long-standing rules. The view is to be 'framed' by trees or traditional buildings, deep perspective and a hint of the unknown beyond are encouraged, buildings merge with the earth, but most signs of contemporary activity are avoided. Not only do people, farm machines and cars vanish from view, but so too do silos, phone and power cables and all but the most traditional roadsigns. Hilder may offer more clarity than Constable but otherwise the view is similar. The point extends to the urban landscape, where Lowry sanctions industrial grime by placing it in the past. All manner of well rehearsed primitives now follow by offering urban and rural scenes where simple people undertake staggering tasks with smiles on their faces. In decorating our living room walls, many opt for a reminder of a world we never lost, an ordered peepshow to the simple life.

Contemporary topographical writing

The main elements of approved topographic description have changed little over the past two hundred years. Travellers in the 18th and 19th centuries spiced their essay descriptions with 'local colour' provided by interviews and insights into life-style, and with historical 'rooting powder' which gave the contemporary view a good chance of being accepted as part of the lineage of local

history. Jan Morris, Ronald Blythe and others are solidly in such a
tradition today. However, oral history, historical reconstruction,
photo essay, and issue-based journeys (with Priestley as the
pioneer) have all accentuated the human content to the detriment
of landscape analysis as descriptive art. This is not surprising, as
one shot from the television camera can transfer the visual image
without any need for language. As a contemporary addition to
topographical 'writing' we therefore have the television spin-off:
stills with elements of script added.

Squatting, eating, hedgerows and 'The Good Life'

The popular television situation comedy 'The Good Life' served
as an apt paradigm for the lifestyle adopted by many in both
country and town who would subscribe to the importance of
landscape in their lives. In order to explore 'The Good Life' (or,
to quote a recent BBC radio title, 'A Small Country Living'),
activities which might be viewed as in consort with the maintenance and enhancement of the rural landscape are set within the
framework of the urban economy. Contemporary rural living or
squatting is presented on television in the same language as are
quaint historical survivals: people, crafts, dialects, landscape
relics. The landscape is thus endorsed as a mystery revealed,
hedgerows can produce food – or at least sufficient for one brave
kitchen experiment or a small batch of wine. But whilst television
coverage may have increased appreciation of rural life and
environments it has also trivialised it, by detaching 'acceptable'
traditions (nut gathering) from necessary actions (chicken
strangling). The living landscape is seldom explored unless one
accidentally turns on the farming programme.

Landscape disintegration on the small screen

The dominance of television images in our lives has reinforced
latent perceptual stereotypes of landscape, especially those of
rural areas:

(a) *The Elgar/'Summer County' (margarine) syndrome.* In com-
     mercials more than in programmes, the rural landscape is so
     elevated as to make the real thing a letdown. Picture the
     'wholesome' food product endorsed by bright sunlight, lush
     green pastures, distant rolling hills, the scrubbed black-and-
     white cattle ambling home, the dialect-prone cloth-capped
     farmer, tile-and-cobble buildings, the scrubbed table, rose-

cheeked wife and smiling children. Over all, Elgar sweeps a star-trail of so-English music. Landscape reality is more likely to be a wet day, Radio 1 on the car stereo, cows delaying a late journey and a distant view cluttered with pylons and dead elms. Television producers take weeks to select an image which we ingest in a few seconds. The landscape has some of the best packaging around, but it is not the product we are meant to buy!

(b) *Landscape as natural history for primary schools.* Nature makes good television, but it is nature in action that grabs the attention, the clever camera technique which throws new light on the natural environment. By focusing on wildlife species or landscape elements, rather than on the ecosystem or the whole landscape, we are encouraged to view the trees rather than the wood. The practical impact is to manipulate species or elements with little recognition of inter-relationships; this is further to demote the significance of landscape seen as more than the sum of parts.

(c) *Always landscape with figures.* Places do not make good television, and buildings even less so. People talk out and play out their functions in place; others then present such functions as the essence of place; and landscape becomes the backdrop for titles, credits and a change of subject. There are some honourable exceptions (Jacquie Burgess's programme on The Fens, several of Betjeman's essays, aspects of Hoskins's television series) but these are few when measured against general television coverage of landscape subjects.

Landscape as the occasion loses out to landscape as incidental

Television has provided opportunities for an impressive range of insights into history, contemporary change, industrial production and invention. Professionals in each area may well claim that in the process it has trivialised each subject and slighted those aspects of most interest to the public at large. In the case of landscape, however, the criticism is rather different: television has simply failed to come to terms with the subject. With values taken from 'Thirties' new photography, landscape has been treated like incidental music, allowed centre stage for effect, but usually treated only as a background element in the presentation. Only with maps, models, sequential diagrams – and much larger air photography and travel budgets – could landscape be made the focus.

Shifting official views

Whereas in the immediate postwar period, new legislation may have been the context within which all discussion of landscape took place, I see the television image as the most important context today. In the remaining sections of this chapter I want to consider official attitudes towards landscape, some aspects of user perceptions, and a few discernible trends which link the professional and public worlds.

The amenity consensus questioned

The guardianship of public 'amenity' is a responsibility that has both vexed and stimulated professional planners in their operation of development control. The postwar landscape has been shaped by this system, and notwithstanding some policy changes (with regard to road form, building materials, permitted uses etc.), the values implicit in development control have, until very recently, maintained the vision proposed in the 'Forties'. Recent proposals would reduce the effective power of planners, placing more responsibility on developer and architect to reflect appropriate design and layout. Although the immediate effect will hardly be evident, cumulative change would be considerable, especially if other elements in the 'Forties' plan for landscape are revised, as in recent disputed proposals for substantial residential communities in London's Green Belt. A few such communities have been permitted on peripheral and 'difficult' sites – as at South Woodham in Essex and Martlesham in Suffolk – but the proposed assault on the Metropolitan Green Belt has revealed that whereas the amenity consensus may have lost some of its edge, certain shared beliefs apparently continue.

Farming landscape or landscape farming

Nowhere are battle-lines over the appropriate image of landscape more firmly drawn than between farming and conservationist interests. The battle has been a continuous one with ultimate victory nearly always going to those who gain their living and, more importantly, their country's food from the land. As with the demolition and replacement of buildings, it is the pace and scale of change, rather than change itself, which generates conflict.

It is now generally recognised that most of the British landscape is man-made and that many localities have undergone significant changes within the lifetimes of older residents. Roads

have been straightened, economically useful woods have reverted
to nature for lack of the woodman's skill, hedges have been
removed, vernacular field buildings have slumped from effective
use to rubble. Those changes have had a cumulative impact on the
landscape, as have the townsman's car, his recreation pursuits,
and his homes. But root out a hedge, burn stubble or fill a pond
and the television reporter descends with simulated wrath learned
at Sir Robin Day's knee. However, with the exception of straw
burning, which has little long-term landscape effect though
immediate impact on suburban washdays, most of the issues
debated are grasped by very few. That today's farmer may
cultivate not only crops and stock, but also landscape through the
'uneconomic' retention and management of hedges, woods,
boundaries, trees and buildings, is little recognised. With advice,
the farmer has often continued the landscape guardianship which
was once exhibited by only the most informed or affluent
landowners.

Managing recreation

But while more of the landscape may be managed so as to
maintain traditional images in the face of economically directed
change, access to that landscape has become much more limited.
By the 'Fifties' car ownership and informal use of rural areas had
led to the relentless growth of measures to control casual rural
use, to meet the complaints expressed by agricultural interests,
Countryside Codes, Commissions and Management Schemes
focused on the reconciliation of various rural interests. Landscape
as such again seems to have taken a back seat in this process.
Selected sites were 'urbanised' so as to offer parking, eating and
other conveniences; chances to explore and contemplate were
replaced by 'views', 'photo-opportunities', 'scenic routes' or
'leisure drives'. Although such terms may be appropriate, they
are emphasised as much for management as for aesthetic purposes. 'Urbanisation' and the interpretation of appropriate sites
package the environmental experience for a willing audience,
with few seeking the traditional informality – and inconvenience
– of personal exploration. Conflicting rural interests are reconciled by segregation: hardly a strategy which would appeal to
urban managers in our multicultural society.

Is there a landscape lobby?

Although a complete list of conservation, rural amenity, natural
history and heritage interest groups would fill the remainder of

this chapter, there is no single focus with high public visibility that concentrates interests on landscape. Rather, such interests are fragmented into countryside, sport, bird life and other separate concerns. Although areas of landscape significance – valued for aesthetic qualities and with clear regional identity – have long been designated; their maintenance has little public visibility. Historical geography and landscape architecture have increasingly sought to explain a wide variety of historic landscapes, but their very scale and visual obscurity seem to have prevented explicit designation. With so much landscape history we in Britain have been less eager than Italy or the United States, for example, to identify specific areas for management. Instead there is a culturally accepted pace of landscape evolution and a deep-rooted recognition of past references in present landscapes. But can we be sure that culturally appropriate landscape(s) will persist without a specific interest group lobbying for them?

Reconciling interests

But what are the perspectives adopted by those using the environment, especially rural areas? Five rather different land-scape activities suggest themselves:

A nice place for making a noise in . . . or, 'why not autocross in a city Sunday parking lot?' Returning to my students' locations for peace and fear, a common set of rural pursuits seems to bridge the two in a strange way by providing immediate danger in a context of surrounding calm. Consider why motor-sports require rural locations? Space and the exclusion of noise from residential areas are two compelling reasons, but if we explore further we might find that the spectator or participant has an appreciation of landscape that is as valid, though less generally accepted, as that of the Sunday painter. The detailed land form of a track or course provides challenge to the participant and viewing excitement to the spectator; the distant view may receive as much attention – in time terms – as it does from the painter. The journey to and from the course, the day's experience, may all provide emotional and recreational opportunities as important as more conventional rural pursuits.

Imbibing and recording. Let me turn another common assumption on its head. Observers and collectors strongly concerned with 'preserving' or 'conserving' the environment might be assumed to have an appreciation and understanding of landscape. But as recent press coverage of ornithology has suggested, the 'collecting' fetish may overcome any concern for context. At best an ecosystem may be considered within a landscape context: at worst species are logged like train numbers, or are actually removed from their environment. Even the majority of concerned observers is more likely to see place as habitat with a marginal aesthetic bonus than as a key element of their experience, to be fully digested.

Reading the Sunday papers.   More likely to regard landscape for its own sake are those strange beings who park in a field entrance or facing an overlooked vista, and use their weighty Sunday paper as a partial retreat from which to contemplate the environment. While many of us continue to be surprised by this behaviour, it is clear that to such visitors the context is very significant, providing the temporary 'room with a view' which may be lacking at home.

Rural pursuits.   Fishing, hunting and some would say camping all offer sophisticated snatches of the age-old battle with nature. Here topography as well as landscape may well be important, and lore and understanding of context are usually integral to the pursuit. The activity itself often seems to compensate for conditions of weather and ground which would dissuade others from ever choosing such a time and place. The landscape as such may be only a happy adjunct to the pursuit itself, though that most popular of sports, fishing, reflects distinct aesthetic divisions between coarse and fly fishing: the latter in more appropriate descent from Walton than the former, where size and weight are all. But it would be wrong to presume widespread landscape, rather than waterscape, awareness amongst fishermen. Of blood sports much could be said and has been said in the traditional literature of the Field, whose similarity to the writing of cricket devotees suggests a learned aesthetic of gentlemanly pursuits rather than any inherent predisposition towards landscape appreciation.

Talking with farmers.   What annoys many conservationists about farmers' expressed attitudes is their apparent callousness and lack of sensitivity towards the natural environment in which they work, and this would indeed be very disturbing were it true. The economics of agriculture have, to some small degree, prised the farmer from his close relationship with the land. Personal experience has been replaced by meters and planting decisions imposed from monitored contracts. But for most farmers the strong tradition of guardianship remains, a tending of inheritance which has, however, always been based on use. The yellow glow of rape in flower is an appreciated visual bonus from a now profitable crop, and if a modern use were found for flax then haze blue would reappear. Footpaths stay open when used and respected, but few farmers support retention of such paths if they are seldom used or if use results in crop damage.

In short, farmers have a language of landscape appreciation – agriculture. It is a living language because it describes a vital activity. The absence of such a language for landscape appreciation in non-agricultural circles may imply the absence of a widespread significant relationship.

Discernible trends

Landscape is never going to feature in any list of top ten public needs; indeed, were it not for the fringe agitators from William Morris to Ian Nairn public discussion on environmental aesthetics would never occur. Scale is so large and descriptors so inadequate as to bar creative public debate. Yet there are current issues and concerns which deserve such debate:

Creating more 'experience' for less landscape. Is there a trend, through open-air museums, designated areas, conserved properties, etc., to encourage a 'drug dependency' which endorses only areas of concentrated landscape and environmental management? How far are we from COTSWORLD or the Wealden Vistaland?

Landscape disputes. The cost-based battle over developments in the landscape will inevitably become aggravated. Discussion based on environmental impact statements will serve only to highlight the paucity of our knowledge when it comes to valuing landscape. Landscape may become fully factorised into uses, carrying-capacity, earning power and habitats unless public language of landscape appreciation is developed.

The landscape 'professions'. Like it or not, landscape architects have cornered the most visible professional responsibility for landscape. The public expects architects to design buildings (though many do not and could not), planners to be able to foresee and ease our path to the future (though few, if any, can) and landscape architects to design and maintain our pleasing areas of arcadia. Though far from successful in meeting public expectations, both architects and planners do have a public voice which pronounces on environmental issues and links the profession with education, public information and the media. In short, both buildings and plans have their lobby. The lobby for that most acceptable of subjects, the landscape, is difficult to discern. Is its potential wasted on such a modest profession as landscape architecture?

'You cannot conquer time'.   I have not dwelt on the age problem in landscape but it may provide the keystone for any public language on the subject. Uncertainty in contemporary society encourages the adoption of very short individual time horizons, and although techniques for destruction (and construction) can make impressive impacts on the landscape in a very short period, the essence of landscape change lies in its unimpeded relationship with the natural life-cycle. Landscape may be sudden birth, as in Spring, or widespread death, as with rabbits or elms, but it is also the strongest tangible image of continuity available to us. True, your view or mine may fill or empty, but elsewhere there will be landscapes – and their recorded images – which we contrive to maintain and mantle with meanings that justify our own short lives. At a time when uncertainty reigns, landscape advocates and managers have a good product to sell.

Future research

Much needs to be done, but much of this was also touched on in 1928:

> It is the duty of the academic world to educate the nation in the appreciation of its heritage of scenery. When the benefits of scenic beauty are thus extended from the few to the many, the people themselves will guard the goodly heritage. The best method for carrying out this instruction in school is in connection with regional survey, for it is almost an epitome of the scenery of the world, comprising the round of day and night, the response of vegetation to the seasons, forms of cloud common to all countries, the rising and setting of the sun and the revolution of the changeless constellations. Moreover, scenery appeals to the mind as a whole, for everything that we know about an object affects the way in which it appears to the eye, yet the feeling imparted by appearance is not limited by the bounds of knowledge.

This proposal from Vaughan Cornish (n.d.) may not set the grant-giving Research Councils reeling but, I would maintain, it provides the basis for the inquiries that we should be pursuing at present. Of course, new words such as 'curriculum', 'environmental education', 'interpretation' and 'visitor management' fit better with public policy and academic concern, but in essence the purpose remains. Three topics deserve attention:

(a) What aspects of landscape evolution, appreciation and management are currently taught in schools?
(b) Has awareness of the benefit of scenic beauty been extended from the few to the many since 1928?
(c) If so, has there been a concomitant strengthening of the guardianship of our landscape heritage?

Landscape education, participation in landscape conservation, and the role of informal and formal conservation strategies are three general themes within which significant, researchable, topics may be identified. No enquiry is more urgent than into the current state of environmental education in this country. We have some environmental education, as well as geography, at the primary and secondary levels, as well as the past support for geography, planning, environmental science – even landscape studies – at the tertiary level. But this may encourage complacency and I fear for all, and each part. Far from being the foundation of environmental education, the 'regional survey' – better now identified as the 'local study' – has been fragmented, largely rejected by geographers, and is, in most cases, devoid of a landscape element at upper educational levels. I realise that this conclusion will open rather than close a discussion and this is precisely my intention. However, it is my hope that in pursuing assertions with regard to the current state of something as tangible as course provision and content, you will also remember that 'the feeling imparted by appearance is not limited by the bounds of knowledge'.

Bibliography

Betjeman, J. 1952. *First and last loves*. London: John Murray.
Betjeman, J. 1973. 'Metro-land'. In *The best of Betjeman*, J. Guest (ed.), pp. 215–36. Harmondsworth: Penguin.
Berger, J. 1972. *Ways of seeing*. London: Penguin/BBC.
Blythe, R. 1969. *Akenfield: portrait of an English village*. London: Allen Lane/The Penguin Press.
Blythe, R. (ed.) 1981. *Places: an anthology*. Oxford: Oxford University Press.

Brandon, P. and R. Millman (eds) 1980. *Recording historic landscapes*, 2 vols. Occasional Publications Series, London: Department of Geography, Polytechnic of North London.

Burgess, J. 1982. 'Filming the Fens: a visual interpretation of regional character'. In *Valued environments*, J. R. Gold and J. Burgess (eds), pp. 35–54. London: Allen & Unwin.

Chappell, W. (ed.) 1982. *A painter remembered by his friends: Edward Burra*. London: André Deutsch Lefevre Gallery.

Cullen, G. 1961. *Townscape*. London: Architectural Press.

Essex County Council 1973. *A design guide for residential areas*. Chelmsford: Essex County Council Planning Department.

Goodey, B. 1977. *Interpreting the conserved environment: issues in planning and architecture*, Working Paper 29. Oxford: Department of Town Planning, Oxford Polytechnic.

Goodey, B. 1979. The interpretation boom. *Area* 11(4), 285–8.

Goodey, B. 1982. Assistance architecturale en région rurale au Royaume Uni: Le 'Essex Design Guide'. In *Assistance en Amenagement de l'Espace*, C. Feltz et al. (eds), pp. 9–20. Arlon: Fondation Roi Baudouin/ Fondation Universitaire Luxembourgeoise.

Goodey, B. 1983. *Houses + promotion = community: the role of media coverage in the creation of place*. Seminar Paper, Media Environments, Institute of British Geographers, Edinburgh, 8 January 1983.

Gutkind, E. A. 1942. Man-made landscape. In *Creative demobilisation: Vol 1. Principles of national planning*, pp. 91–119. London: Kegan Paul, Trench, Trubner & Co.

Hawkins, J. and M. Hollis, 1979. *Thirties: British art and design before the War*. London: Arts Council of Great Britain.

Hoskins, W. G. 1955. *The making of the English landscape*. London: Hodder & Stoughton.

Jarvis, B. 1983. *Readers, travellers, visitors, inhabitants and storytellers: notes for an existential urban design*. Gloucestershire Papers in Local and Rural Planning 18, Gloucester: Department of Town and Country Planning, Gloucester College of Art and Design.

Jeffrey, I. 1979. Photo-journalism: feeling for the past. In: *Thirties: British art and design before the War*, pp. 109–20. London: Arts Council of Great Britain.

Jeffrey, I. 1983. Public problems and private experience in British art and literature. In: *Landscape in Britain 1850–1950*. London: Arts Council of Great Britain.

Lowe, P. and J. Goyder, 1983. *Environmental groups in politics*. London: Allen & Unwin.

Nairn, I. 1975. Outrage 20 years after. *Architectural Review*, December, 328–37.

Priestley, J. B. 1933. *English journey*. London: Gollancz.

Sontag, S. 1978. *On photography*. New York: Delta.

Sontag, S. 1982 (edn) Against interpretation. In: *A Susan Sontag reader*, E. Hardwick (ed.). Harmondsworth: Penguin.

Vaughan Cornish (n.d.) The preservation of scenic beauty in town and country. *Geographical essays*, 73–9. London: Sifton, Praed & Co. (paper delivered 1928).

Weller, J. B. *et al.* 1976. Rural settlement and landscape. *Architects' Journal*, 21 January, 1976.

Williams, R. 1975. *The country and the city*. London: Paladin.

Critiques and queries

The points raised below have been selected from the overtly critical comments on Brian Goodey's chapter, to show the diversity of opinion on the topic.

Dick Watson   This contribution fizzes with life. It is a fresh and stimulating approach to the subject which sets out to provoke thought and (I think) disagreement. Brian Goodey has interesting and disparaging things to say about the use of landscape in advertising, about the 'packaging' of landscape, and about superficial approaches to landscape. Certain of the modern developments which are questioned here may be more valuable than the writer suggests (e.g. recreational uses, picnic sites: many people *do* feel inexplicably better for 'a run in the car' on Sunday afternoon). Advertising usage of landscape may be deplorable, but it does recognise an ideal somewhere: this may be escapist, or fugitive, but is it entirely wrong to wish for it?

Meanwhile I am suspicious of the olde-England wool-spinning and goat-milking bit. It continues to survive in spite of what Evelyn Waugh did to it in *Put out more flags*. And how good is the National Trust in preserving the country's heritage? For whom does it function, primarily? Who are its members? I also question the implication that there is something similar in Constable and Hilder. There isn't, in one vital respect: Constable was *first*. Also he and Turner have plenty of human activity in their painting – too much, one sometimes thinks, in Turner's case.

Stephen Daniels   Brian Goodey addresses the issues of 'meanings and values in landscape' directly and provocatively. He addresses the critical question of the *language* of landscape interpretation. There is indeed a 'dreadful poverty' to the ordinary language of landscape interpretation and scarcely more riches in the language of professionals and academics. I would like to see a more adequate analysis of the *social history* of the language of landscape.

Goodey's historical understanding seems to stop in the 1930s.

He raises the important question of political ideology; the politics of landscape is conservative. The conventional idea of landscape obscures as it soothes and delights. The association with 'heritage' is revealing. Heritage is ruling class history and (as Hobsbawm and Ranger show in *The invention of tradition*) much is deliberately created to give the illusion of continuity. Goodey seems to subscribe to this ideology despite his playfully ironic attitude. 'At a time when uncertainty reigns', he tells us on page 96, 'landscape advocates and managers have a good product to sell'. Like the Royal Wedding, landscape obscures our view of troubling economic and moral issues. Once it could comprehend them.

Ian Laurie I believe landscape interpretation, advocated by Brian Goodey, assists awareness and understanding of landscape and its meanings and values. It is a desirable aid but it has responsibilities and limitations not always recognised by the 'interpreter' as an informer and conditioner of public opinions and attitudes.

Muriel Laverack Brian Goodey says there is an inadequate language of landscape appreciation. Most of the time those in practice, academic circles, lobbies (even consumers?) understand each other well enough. If a 'landscape language' were ever agreed it would (a) be a long time ahead, (b) tend to stultify, and (c) need a translator.

This is the paper which struck most notes of recognition and understanding with me, but also the one in which I most often reject the logic or conclusion. One of Brian Goodey's themes is that there *is* an English landscape taste, but it lacks a basis for maintaining and managing this charm capsule because it lacks an adequate common language. The logic of that escapes me and I have not myself found language the main barrier to understanding or to incremental success.

'Control' is too strong a word for the reaction to recreation and access – 'influencing', 'educating', 'enhancing experience', 'managing resources' . . . Do I detect a slight sneer at the packaged environmental experience in comparison with the traditional informal personal exploration? Some would say the latter smacks of elitism and the prewar consumption of remoteness, grandeur and romanticism. In the postwar situation of affluence, leisure and mobility, many would rather go to the landscaped car park, the visitor centre, the interpreted nature trail. Some can still go up the mountain, and perhaps be glad that most of the rest do not want to. Again I fail to see the basis of the argument that it is absence of a public language of landscape appreciation which inhibits the enjoyment of understanding and personal exploration and elevates the creation of 'experiences'.

Ian Brotherton   Brian Goodey appears to have a love–hate relationship with television, suggesting that landscape appreciation must be developed through it. Is he concerned at the values being promoted or the media takeover of landscape? Television must have introduced many facets of landscape to many people. And modern life must expose more people to more landscapes both real and portrayed than hitherto. His paper appears unbalanced by omitting this side of things, but it is interesting and encouraging to see the links with Craik's analysis.

Brian Goodey replies: A re-reading of my chapter requires that I state quite clearly that it was intended to provoke seminar discussion, rather than to serve as a printed statement of purpose.

I am preoccupied with 20th-century culture, with the impact of media images, and design guidance in Essex. On balance I am *for* all of these, although not uncritical of their development and impact. I also believe that visitor management and interpretation are essential from the perspective both of conservation and of environmental education; nevertheless excesses of enthusiasm in these areas deserve criticism.

My comments on the role of farmers as conservationists were overstated in order to achieve a debate (which has not emerged). I am unwilling to revise my observations on landscape architecture, but am rather more convinced than most of the utility of fox hunting as a perverted form of horse, and landscape, conservation.

7 The delights and problems of practice

HAL MOGGRIDGE

Introduction

Changing the landscape is a characteristic of the human species. Perhaps at first a desire to make land more productive or comfortable may have motivated deliberate changes, as a beaver builds a dam to provide local conditions which suit it. But human self-consciousness leads on to a poetic appreciation of the emotional effects of landscape upon people, an awareness which has inevitably culminated in attempts to evoke emotional responses through landscape design.

Making and shaping landscapes gives satisfaction and enjoyment to those who undertake it. Indeed, as much satisfaction seems to be derived by those whose motives are wholly extractive as by those who perceive their work on the landscape as creative in intention. The individual who ruthlessly pushes away a bosky mountainside in order to extract an ore from within it appears to derive the same emotional pleasure from contemplating the landscape despoiled by his activity as that enjoyed by the renovator who revives a spoil tip from shapeless sterility into a fair and living landscape. The purposes of the two may have been opposite and the benefits of their activities disparate, the former obtaining wealth from the land, the latter beauty and life. None the less, some equally basic joy appears to be derived from reshaping the land; the smile which lights the face of a child playing in a sand pit lies deep in the heart of the adult.

In the same way, growing things from the land seems to offer opportunities for satisfaction regardless of the end motive. A crop may be seen simply as a source of money, and the ostensible reason for raising it may be greed, sometimes sufficient even to justify degradation of the soil. More fundamentally, the crop may be food essential to survival in the coming year. On the other hand, plants may be grown for pleasure in their beauty as they unroll colour, texture and fragrance, shining in the sun and rain. Yet all the people involved with growing these plants, whatever their purpose, can enjoy a like satisfaction in the craftsmanship of the process. Similarly designers, in imagining and initiating a future landscape, are rewarded by their activity rather than by its morality of purpose.

Yet the day-to-day effort of changing the landscape may also seem to be nothing but a series of painful experiences, mishaps and struggles. The designer is harried by the changing whims and budgets of his client, by the disorderly demands of everyday life, by his own inability to explain or control his imagination, by lack of information about technical matters and by perpetual questions and deadlines. The craftsman has to contend with continuous bad weather – possibly only an hour intervening between waterlogging and drought – with confused and changing instructions, with the impossibility of obtaining materials and equipment and many other difficulties in achieving any of the results required. Indeed, when practitioners meet, they tend to discuss their activity in terms of case studies and techniques rather than theories. Designers perceive the landscape itself simultaneously as a precious reality and as a field of action across which their imaginations and activities will range, stimulating capabilities for change and creativity.

A cartoon of a designer's conception of landscape

A landscape designer, then, is one who seeks to initiate and control change in the landscape, usually for purposes determined by others. Therefore landscape is perceived in terms of malleability. It may be described as consisting of a series of elements, each changing through time at a different speed, like a slowed-down version of images moving across the screen of some electronic game. Various objects of differing size and colour move randomly at different speeds, and the game consists of action within the disciplines imposed by these various movements.

The slowest object, perceived as permanent, is the screen itself; this is like our planet, the Earth. We know that both screen and Earth are slowly decaying towards a state in which the game itself will cease to exist. This level of decay is beyond human control except in so far as we seek to make sure that we do not damage the screen or the machine which holds it. To play the game by striking the screen with a hammer would be catastrophic – the very game itself might not be renewable.

Some objects move slowly across the screen. Geological timescales leading to major land formation are too slow for human beings to control. Only localised and sudden geological catastrophes, such as the results of landslips, can be reproduced by human agency. These often change the physical characteristics of the subsoil and sweep away the surface characteristics of the land. However, because they are rapid they are accessible to human action. But they are the sole point at which humans impinge upon the geological process.

Other landscape processes are more accessible to human interference and creativity. The formation of living soils and mosaics of vegetation, though still operating at a pace much slower than a single human life-span, are perceptible and alterable within a lifetime. Individual plants and animals vary in their life-spans from the centuries-long ageing of an oak tree to the brief timespan of a wasteland annual or fruit fly. Climatic phenomena can be so fast yet so powerful that humans can do no more than modify the way in which they occur; wind can be softened, water diverted, sunlight brought into view in the instant of its passage.

To make action possible – and landscape practice is action – elements of the landscape which cannot be remoulded tend to be ignored. Those who aim at a single-minded remodelling of land will bother only with the swiftest natural cycles. Open-cast mining can shift aside the living surface crust of the land, exposing the mineral to be extracted by controlling erosion by water, wind and gravity. The crudest design intentions will be satisfied even if the completed landscape is a sterile, but stable, slag heap; only an Aberfan disaster is a failure in these terms. Somewhat more far-sighted is the agriculturalist who pushes aside and stores the top layer of soil in advance and respreads it over the shaped spoil afterwards to provide grazing for farm animals. More subtle landscape design may develop procedures that ultimately create a new landscape. This may include both a rich variety of life-cycles, for instance pioneer woodlands with herbs on infertile soils, or arable fields on deep, well-structured soils, and elements intended to satisfy aesthetic responses to the fall of light and the shape of ground and vegetation in silhouette.

Yet all these levels of design sophistication may ignore an intricate, slowly developing element like a bluebell wood or an eyecatching clump of trees a century old, either deliberately to permit a desired change or through crudity of perception and knowledge. Landscape design should also include protectiveness towards those parts of the landscape which cannot be remade

within the time-span of human foresight; we should protect what
we cannot ourselves remake.

Landscape design is a process of rearranging interacting forces.
These are many and complex, including for instance: landform;
water, still or flowing; earth as a life force; genius loci; vegetation,
its mass, texture, colour, tempo of growth and decay; climate,
affecting the comfort of fauna and vegetation; light, perception,
intervisibility; movement patterns of fauna including man;
human settlements; artificial land surfaces.

No one individual can possibly understand all these subjects.
Yet when their interrelationships are subjected to rapid change,
the designer seeks to imagine and bring into being a new life-
enhancing landscape which encompasses all possibilities, even
those which are not comprehended.

Purposes of shaping landscape

Human beings shape their landscapes for many different purposes, each influencing the way in which the land is evaluated.

(a) *Economic*. The land is the source of primary production.
Raw materials providing energy and metals are extracted
from it. Food is grown on it. When these products are
evaluated in terms of money, the landscape itself is seen in
monetary values; the physical character of the landscape then
becomes secondary to its value as a productive resource. The
activity of using raw materials produces unwanted materials.
These are wasted and are returned to the land.

The influence of this basic, simple view of landscape upon
human action is considerable. Wars are fought and fortunes
_xchanged to satisfy economic demands made on land.
Many animals also appear to apprehend land in this way and
to struggle with others for possession of territory.

(b) *Practical*. There are many other practical uses of landscape
besides production measurable as money. As birds create
nests so people make places for habitation and all the
activities associated with living. Vegetation and structures
are arranged to shelter much-used places from excessive
wind or sun, to create localised microclimates more comfortable than the regional climate and to provide privacy.
The land is shaped according to the needs of a multiplicity of
land uses, various types of sport and recreation, outdoor
storage, meeting places, places to sit and to stand. The

surface of the land is riddled with communication routes, footpaths, pavements, roads, canals, railways and pipes.

The efficient provision of facilities for this multiplicity of functions is sometimes put forward as the principal purpose of landscape design. The result is measurable in terms of the identifiable responses of users whose satisfaction is sought.

(c) *Aesthetic.*   Landscapes evoke emotions from human beings. These may arise from responses derived from human evolution, responses that are recognised even when the reason for them remains mysterious. They may be the result of historical association and memory. They may be related to the cultural ideas of a particular period or civilisation. They may simply be pleasure in things well made and well cared for – human craftsmanship.

Some such aesthetic responses seem to be transitory, others persistent. It is no longer comprehensible that 200 years ago play-acting hermits with shaggy hair and clothes in small huts should have evoked genuine feelings of melancholy and awe. On the other hand, contrived 'natural' pictures of temples set amongst trees beside water still strike a chord of response even from those who know nothing of classical allegory. Certain aesthetic responses persist across time and culture. A new classical temple in Milton Keynes would seem inconceivable; yet a Buddhist shrine has been built by a lake there, and serves essentially the same scenic role.

Many respond emotionally in certain ways to created landscapes without being able to specify consciously why they do so. Indeed the reasons put forward often seem to be more transitory than the response. Few today would accept that a certain curve is a line of beauty which must give pleasure. Yet landscape created on the basis of such curves continues to delight, sometimes even when the curves themselves have become irregular and overgrown. Complex emotions can be generated by deliberate creations even though the creator does not understand why such combinations of form and texture induce them. Burke needed to call on associations of ideas to express the feeling of beauty:

> Most people must have observed the sort of sense they have had of being swiftly drawn in an easy coach on a smooth turf, with gradual ascents and declivities. This will give a better idea of the Beautiful than almost anything else.

Strangely, this comparison remains evocative today even amongst those who have never actually been 'drawn in an easy coach'.

The well tempered landscape

A landscape described as 'well designed' is likely to be one which evokes aesthetic response while also satisfying economic and practical purposes, its multiplicity of uses all co-ordinated with an integrated whole. For this reason single-purpose landscapes, for instance those designed solely for transport, forestry or horticultural display, tend to be unsatisfactory except to the direct beneficiaries. Equally, solely aesthetic purposes rarely outlive changes of taste from one generation to the next. Experience from the past shows that well tempered landscapes can be created, although by what process remains a mystery. Those who seek to do so tend to discuss their activities in terms of the practical problems encountered in making changes. It is as if the delights and problems of practice are more comprehensible and interesting to practitioners than its results!

Some scholars, by contrast, seek to explain how landscapes were made in the past in terms of a ruthless rationality. Such a tendency towards determinism discounts the significance of the landscape maker's own whims, which derived from many valuable and subtle influences on the individual. Deterministic theories do indeed help to explain the impact of economic and practical influences on the landscape. But we should not underestimate the contribution of conscious human craftsmanship and ideas on the character of the landscape.

Great imaginations have designed some great landscapes. The artistic contribution of men such as Vignola, le Nôtre or Brown is indisputable. That deliberate aesthetic motivation can influence landscape change is not in question. But the work of such acknowledged artists is rarely, if ever, discussed in terms also of the practical contribution of their designs to efficient and economic land use. Yet it seems false to discuss Brown's work entirely in terms of the aesthetics of the English landscape movement, when his own master plans contain schedules mainly of practical functions. His 1771 plan of Lowther Park, for instance, contains the following key:

> A. The House
> B. A Place for the Offices
> C. A place for the Courts to ditto
> D. A Greenhouse
> E. A Place for the Flower Garden
> F. Menagerie
> G. Sunk Fence
> H. Approach to the House

I.   Kitchen Garden
K.   Flues
L.   Hot Walls
M.   Fire Places for the Flues
N.   Espaliers
O.   Melon Ground
P.   Stoves

Eleven of these 15 facilities are practical land uses related to the support of the population that depends on the estate for its livelihood. This is not to assert that Brown was not greatly concerned with aesthetics; merely that he also valued efficiency and productivity.

Conversely, the extension of aesthetic ideas into the landscape at large is often not acknowledged. That ordinary mortals could have designed and shaped their landscapes with the same sort of combination of aesthetic and practical sensibility as great masters of design is not given credibility. Yet it is under this combination of influences that effective practice is carried out today. So why not in the past, whose created landscapes often still satisfy us?

To cite an example: Mr Isaac of Geufron Farm, near Ysbyty Ystwyth, has accounted for the presence of a rowan tree in the middle of a reclaimed field on his farm with the explanation that each time he ploughed or sprayed he worked round the tree because of the pleasure the tree gave him. No doubt it was originally self-set; but the aesthetic pleasure of the farmer nursed it to maturity. In the adjoining parish, the Countryside Commission's Upland Landscapes Study asked all the farmers to identify the landscape they considered most beautiful in their parish. By far the best-loved landscape was the valley of the Ystwyth and the Hafod estate, planted and landscaped by Thomas Johnes, friend of Uvedale Price and cousin of Payne Knight, over one and a half centuries earlier. The famous house and park have since gone. But the careful aesthetic composition of these outlying parts of the designed landscape still appeals to the majority; is it not likely that they may have wished to create comparable effects on their own farms?

Those who shape the landscape probably always assume that a satisfyingly designed landscape will unite economic, practical and aesthetic values in a single composition. Designers of beautiful landscapes are also apt to assume that the desire to attain such satisfaction is widespread amongst humanity. They arrogantly claim for themselves as practitioners some instinctive knowledge of human motivation. They do not, and indeed dare not, question this assumption too closely, for too much consideration can lead to excessive caution and so to inaction – the opposite of practice.

Some research needs

Practitioners are likely to favour research which could provide techniques for diagnosing and solving the problems of practice. Users may prefer that research should equip practitioners with greater awareness of how landscape is used and perceived. Both will be needed within any satisfactory overall framework of landscape research. The latter type is likely to be thought nearer to academic interests and so may receive greater support. This would be an error. Pragmatic research which leads directly to more skilful practice should be highly valued; although it may not extend the boundaries of human knowledge, it can lead to bettering the real environment in which people live.

Before landscape research can be launched with a coherent framework, preliminary work is required so that research can be applied to assist practice.

(a) *Collating existing experience and knowledge.* Much of the background information guiding landscape practice is based on generalisations derived from specific examples. Although these examples may be accurately assessed they are not necessarily adequate bases for general conclusions. Knowlege acquired at random by past research and practice now needs to be collected together and collated to guide future action effectively.

(b) *An internationally agreed terminology.* If knowledge is to be exchanged or processed coherently, perhaps by computers, the meaning of terminology must be defined and agreed. Many words are used differently by different disciplines or in different eras. For instance a 'tent' in the 18th century would be called a 'marquee' today. A 'pavement' in the USA is a 'road' in Britain. The word 'wilderness' has been narrowed by ecologists into a specific scientific definition of a certain type of land, whereas national park authorities use it to describe the emotional impact of a wide range of landscapes upon visitors. As Gerard Manley Hopkins writes, 'O let them be left, wildness and wet; Long live the weeds and the wilderness yet'. It matters less which definitions become authoritative than that energy should not be wasted arguing about the meanings of terms.

(c) *Practical skills, knowledge and examples.* The practitioner's conception of the landscape and his desire to find means of solving practical problems suggest that more knowledge along the following lines would improve performance:

(i) Down-to-earth understanding of the *existing landscape* and how it works needs ever to be improved.

(ii) Some landscapes should be *conserved* from change. These may include historical, vernacular, and ancient natural landscapes and landscapes so stable in character that they cannot be remade. *Historic landscapes* are the indispensable library of the landscape practitioner, and the National Heritage Act of 1983 encourages the collection of historical landscape records. Better knowledge of what elements are really irreplaceable, and an over-all evaluation of landscapes which should be conserved is required.

(iii) If historical landscapes are to be conserved they must be *maintained*. For this purpose vernacular techniques and skills must be understood. Such skills may prove useful in solving future practical problems too. Yet the vernacular crafts both from town and country are at present slipping out of use unrecorded. An accurate record of them in comprehensive terms is needed. This technical record will also revive a once vital language: for instances the 'framard', 'drawing knife', 'half shell bit' and 'tomahawk': all tools used for hurdle-making.

(iv) Knowledge about *how to regenerate complex associations of vegetation* is being increased rapidly by trial and error and by theoretical study. This knowledge now needs to be brought together in an authoritative way. Then theoretical study followed by field trials should be initiated to enable complex landscapes built up only under natural conditions to be re-established effectively by man within a much shorter time.

(d) *Knowledge of practical landscape uses.* The practical uses of landscape are still understood only in an elementary way. Many aspects which would lead to safer and more satisfying landscapes need more study. To cite concrete examples:

(i) Though it is known that steps built out of doors need to be differently proportioned than those made inside buildings, comfortable relationships between riser, tread and width have not been authoritatively assessed;

this could be done first on the basis of field trials, without trying to explain why certain proportions are comfortable and safe.

(ii) Safety on small roads is poorly understood. How is it that Italian towns, which feel so hazardous to both pedestrians and driver, have one of the lowest accident rates per mile in Europe? Why is motor insurance in Cornwall, with its narrow, blind lanes, lower than elsewhere?

(iii) The capacity of different types of landscape to withstand wear-and-tear clearly differs. Precise guidance on capacity is needed in terms both of physical ground conditions and of the psychology of distance and crowding.

(e) *Aesthetic aspects of landscape design.* In an age which tends to doubt the importance of aesthetic reactions or their influence on social behaviour, research into the aesthetic aspects of landscape design is as important as the more directly practical knowledge touched on above. The practitioner will want this research to result in guidance which is useful on the drawing board and the site. Do those who shape and those who use the landscape perceive it differently? The following theories might be put to the test:

(i) The assertion made above that the whole British landscape has evolved under influences which include a conscious search for beauty and comfort should be examined. At the same time the theory that almost everyone perceives and values beauty in the landscape around him can be examined – some work on this subject has already been carried out in the USA.

(ii) Techniques for touching human emotions when making, modifying and maintaining landscapes need to be defined. 'L' aged 16 of Sevenoaks in the booklet *Ask the Kids* shows how important this is:

'There should places of darkness and of light, of grass and of earth. . . . We used to stare out of the window, and because there were no irregularities to stimulate us, we stayed inside.'

How can designers foresee how people are likely to perceive and hence react to their creations? It might be sensible to start with Repton's work, update it and enlarge upon it.

(iii) Satire and humour have played a part in landscape design for several centuries, from the weird attributes of Vignola's Villa Orsini at Bomarzo to Disneyland. What amuses us in a profound way?

(iv) The early garden festivals in Germany were apparently based upon the assumption that fine landscapes could improve morale and social cohesion. To that end, while Stuttgart was still suffering the after-effects of bombardment, the centre of the city was rejuvenated. Can studies be devised to test whether such improvement really restores the self-confidence as well as the physical fabric of a desolate inner city? If so, what sorts of landscape work are most effective?

Listing these possible subjects for research leads to the conclusion that man's relationship to nature is as yet hardly understood. Where definable understanding is lacking, then the instincts of artistic perception become the best guide to invention. Research which leads to practical means of sharpening and using these instincts in practice must be worthwhile.

Critiques and queries

The comments below principally highlight the main critical analyses of the paper, to show the divergence of views and assessments of the landscape field.

Stephen Daniels The chapter is a sobering insight into the day-to-day down-to-earth practicalities of landscape design; it should be required reading for high-minded students of landscape gardening. But can landscapes in cities improve the happiness and morale of the inhabitants, as Hal Moggridge asks? A study of Victorian park design should make us suspect this question since there was a strong connotation of social control to such ideas of morale and happiness, and perhaps there still is. Whose morality are we talking about? Are parks happier places than pubs?

Ian Laurie Fine humanised landscapes cannot be, in my view, successfully re-modelled without harnessing artistic sensibility and skills. Intuition and imagination are essential skills for a good designer and good design gives value for money spent on it when it becomes widely appreciated by those who use it and see it. Intuition is of course inadequate as the sole basis for good design.

Dick Watson This is a very interesting paper, although it is evidently the work of a good-tempered individual, and I think it could have been more severe. It could have said more strongly, for instance, that certain activities actually destroy landscape. Most of these are concerned with money.

The assertion that an individual who pushes away a 'bosky mountainside' derives an emotional pleasure from this seems to me to be an extraordinarily charitable way of putting it. Such an individual derives a pleasure, first, from making pots of money and, secondly, from destroying things, much as psychopaths enjoy pulling wings off insects.

What is missing from this discussion is the sense of wickedness. I use this word rather in the old-fashioned sense of *sin* (a word we think of too rarely these days: the destruction of landscape is one of the things which persuades me to believe in Original Sin) and a Christian would say that mankind is the custodian of God's Creation and has a duty to see it properly.

What Moggridge neglects, I think, is the evil selfishness of generations of landowning gentry, the Dukes who own Belgravia and Mayfair, and those who ruined Nottinghamshire and County Durham (not to mention enslaving their inhabitants). Those people demonstrate that one attitude to landscape can be that which is totally without responsibility, consideration, or care. Society has, of course learned from them, and their rottenness has spread: to ruthless estate-builders, factory-farmers, and litter-louts. All these anti-landscape people are merely copying the example of the English nobility and landed gentry. The Aberfan disaster is directly attributable to a centuries-old practice of using the landscape to make money.

8 Themes, speculations and an agenda for landscape research

EDMUND C. PENNING-ROWSELL

The preceding Chapters 2 to 7 present six individual perspectives on landscape meanings and values. They are idiosyncratic and designed to provoke rather than reconcile. The critiques and queries that follow each chapter are also intended to show how diverse the views of different commentators can be within a common field of interest.

In discussion, of course, we become more concerned with understanding another's viewpoint than with advocating our own particular positions. We search for common ground, seek a harmony of opinion, and attempt to reach broad conclusions that can comfortably accommodate a range of perspectives.

This chapter presents a synthesis of these working party discussions. It shows a diversity of views collected around four themes, each of which bridges the subject matter of the previous chapters. Innumerable unanswered and perhaps unanswerable questions remain. These show our ignorance rather than our knowledge, and this chapter also attempts to assemble from these questions at least some of the essential items that might appear on a landscape research agenda for the future.

Landscape experience and perception

The meanings we comprehend and the values we hold about landscape appear to be intimately connected with the way we perceive landscapes and this in turn appears to relate to our landscape experiences. However, in research and commentary landscape has usually been regarded as separate and distant: out there' rather than as part of ourselves. The emphasis has thus been put on perception *of* landscapes rather than experience *in* landscapes, and on landscape merely as an impersonal assemblage of visible features rather than a realm of interaction.

Landscape perception is concerned with using, remembering and learning. Nevertheless our perceptions are distorted: features are emphasised rather than views, landscape rather than scenes, 'countryside' rather than 'landscape'. There is a conflict between objectifying landscape – which we feel we need for deepening our understanding – and attitudes to landscape as part of life. The mismatch between scientific curiosity and personal prejudices gives rise to tensions in us as researchers and persons.

Questions abound. How are habits of perception or seeing developed? How malleable are they? Can a person 'escape' from his or her innate perspective into different ways of seeing landscape? How can we analyse a sense of place without destroying its quintessentially unanalysable character? How do the perceptions and affections of those with a background in landscape studies differ from those who have not?

Landscapes also carry symbolic meanings that are not so wholly innocent as might at first be thought. Created landscapes can be assertions of power – over nature or over neighbours – and our cognition of landscapes is selective and sometimes deliberately distorted in the pursuit of our own interests. Landscapes may have an ideological function in mystifying rather than revealing: confusing by distortion or other emphases, rather than providing simple and accessible patterns. Thus our ways of seeing and knowing (perception and cognition) are influenced by the social relations inherent in the landscapes we view. Testing this empirically is difficult but historical evidence shows, for example, how 18th-century landscape gardens and parks were created as expressions of political (Whig) dominance. In a similar way grouse moors and farmed landscapes are expressions of capitalist society today, and city landscapes are manipulated to proclaim the loudest social messages.

Thus perception and cognition are inseparable from experience and from landscape use. But how does familiarity create affection for or indifference to landscapes? What precise associations do different landscapes convey? Some landscapes provide, for example, a sense of health – they signify places where we can be fit. The Countryside Commission research on the meaning that countryside held for 'ordinary people' showed that visual aspects were hardly mentioned: peace, quiet, health and the contrast with the everyday environment were all-important. Other surveys show that we generally do not separate aesthetic judgements from questions of landscape use, in part perhaps because aesthetic judgements are so poorly developed in our education.

We do know that landscape contrasts, even within cities, are of paramount importance in raising consciousness. Anticipation likewise heightens awareness, experience and perception. The contrast between dramatic landscapes and everyday environments also heightens appreciation: it provides the drama of surprise. What we do not know is the extent to which those from different cultural backgrounds share our consciousness and sense of place. A person from, say, Malawi might only view a landscape in his or her economic terms, as a source for food, not as an aesthetically pleasurable experience. Furthermore most people in Britain and the USA do not live in wild landscapes, as do those from more remote parts of the world. They therefore experience landscapes from afar, not as an intimate context to their prosperity or survival, and this surely affects their experience and appreciation, although precisely how is little understood.

The power that landscape has over people may differ widely. We think of the profit from agriculture, of the historical associations from heritage land, the community significance of common land, the privacy of gardens and parks. Other landscapes are shaped for social control: parkland walls to deter intruders or the greening of cities (Liverpool) to placate social unrest. Each landscape has a different message but each relates to the social context of that land use: the power relations behind the visual phenomena.

Values and tradition are clearly crucial to landscape meanings. American and English concepts of landscape are often assumed to be homogenous but the English view is closely tied in with *heritage* whereas the American perspective links more closely with *environment*; England has LANDSCAPE, the USA just landscape. Landscape values generally appear to focus on the past, rather than on potential landscape innovations. New landscapes are distrusted. This is perhaps because, in Brinck Jackson's terms, we are losing the vernacular and gaining the political landscape, with its implications of distance and coercion which we distrust and dislike. Our attitudes towards landscape are static and preservationist. We hope the landscapes we love will endure, despite the pressures we also put on them; we seek stability rather than change. Nevertheless our knowledge of the values or tastes leading to different landscape preferences is sparse, and we know little even about how to analyse them.

Preference and taste

Taste fundamentally affects landscape attitudes and aspirations.

Our patterns of preferences and prejudices arise from our backgrounds, our education, and also can be imposed from 'above' by political systems and social institutions. However our knowledge of taste is dominated by impressions from literate people – little is known about 'mass taste': the everyday taste of everyone.

The formation of 'taste'

The fundamental questions – other than 'what exactly is taste?' – are how taste is formed, what variety in taste is there and why, and what socialisation processes form the landscape tastes we now have? These questions dominate our discussions of landscape taste, and there are few universally acceptable answers.

Preferences and prejudices could derive from a hierarchy of elements: biological characteristics; social systems; personal characteristics. Biologists stress the biological bases of behaviour – as in Gordon Orians's theories of savanna landscapes informing current preferences – whereas psychologists stress the role of personality differences, hence Kenneth Craik's suggestions for personality assessments of key landscape designers and managers. Others see the foundation of preferences as part socially determined by cultural milieu and part biologically influenced. The controversy over biological theories of behaviour rages perhaps because they threaten people's feeling that they have their own independent ideas.

Whatever its determinants, the question remains: how much in landscape taste is universal and how much diversity is there? Until the end of the eighteenth century everything connected with taste was seen as uniform: taste referred to 'nature' and 'human nature' was everywhere the same. Only with post-mercantilist colonisation did an awareness of diversity emerge, made manifest by the demonstrable differences of culture and taste seen in distant lands. Thus we now recognise a plethora of influences on landscape preferences and prejudices: history; culture; social class; landscape function or use; personality and, perhaps, our biological base. What is needed is some form of conceptual map to help classify this maze of influences, and perhaps some mechanism or insight with which to weigh their various significances.

Moreover, taste also implies both 'good taste' and 'bad taste'. Good taste is conservative (if not Conservative) and the images of landscape conventionally considered most significant are often travesties of reality. The scenes are nostalgically mis-interpreted as in the 'Hay Wain' chocolate box stereotype: 'history in soft focus'. These nostalgic views are not just those of middle-class National Trust preservationists; they appear to satisfy needs throughout the social spectrum: '*The diary of an Edwardian lady*' and other historical reconstructions make a link with the past that has near-universal appeal. However such views are a force against change and fail to recognise the sometimes unattractive reality of the landscapes Constable painted and others that are likewise revered. Nevertheless what has previously been considered as 'bad taste' is now in fashion – protected petrol filling stations – as an indication that taste is not static but dynamic and often unpredictable.

The role of the artist

Art articulates feelings of which we were previously unaware, and these feelings in turn modify the way we think about landscapes. Historically, artists have influenced landscape taste such that people now expect paintings to be representational – as are landscape paintings – and the taste for landscape paintings has never waned completely, hence the difficulties we have with 'modern' art. But how far do artists themselves form our taste, and how much do critics and galleries? What process informs a shift in artists' interests? How does taste change; who decides?

Artists also attempt to bring excitement to mere scenery, with bright colours or outlandish combinations. 'Scientific' assessments of landscape preferences may under-rate the excitement of a landscape and the pleasures of surprise and activity. Unusual vistas, surprising use of water, fountains, tree-shapes and statues can all give delight. Landscape designers can try to replicate such excitement – especially in children's playgrounds – but conventional good taste eschews such experiments except in 'theme parks'.

Art should articulate insights to make actual landscapes more accessible to our understanding. Our view of Suffolk landscapes is now inseparable from Constable's paintings, which have helped to highlight the landscape's appeal. In Constable's time, however, his paintings described working landscapes, not a rural idyll; historical reality is distorted or simply ignored in our appreciation now of both the paintings and the landscape. Lowry's scenes of industrial Manchester have highlighted environmental qualities not previously appreciated. Formal reactions have followed, such as the designation of urban conservation areas, showing the power of artists to raise awareness and affect policy.

Variety in preferences and prejudices

We know little in a systematic fashion about different people's landscape tastes – most of our knowledge is anecdotal. Different age groups and different classes do appear to have different aspirations. Young people see landscapes as places for activity: the BMX landscape, dangerous and therefore exciting. The old seek peace and repose. But many people say they want 'peace' when they visit the countryside but then visit the places most popularly visited. The preferences and prejudices of children may thus be more similar to those of adults than we suppose.

Landscape tastes vary with context as well as with culture. Brinck Jackson suggests that wilderness represents 'freedom' rather than 'contact with Nature' to 'blue collar' and working-class people. Middle-class visitors, on the other hand, regard it as a place to be analysed scientifically or in which to behave in a prescribed 'cultural' way.

Familiarity with landscapes also moulds our tastes. Compared with local residents visitors appear to have different landscape aspirations, often created by artists or novelists ('the Bronte country'). We are thus preconditioned with expectations and preferences from literature and painting: how important then, is surprise? Nevertheless we know little about those expectations or the extent to which they are a product of knowledge of how landscapes have evolved and how they are designed. Examining the differences between taste and our simple initial definition of it as patterns of preferences and prejudices might be a useful way forward here.

Description and persuasion

Interdisciplinary discussion of landscape highlights problems of language and terminology. Brian Goodey suggests that the poverty of landscape description inhibits expression and understanding. Such inhibitions carry implications about our education in landscape matters and the role of the media in creating a vocabulary of landscape analysis and appreciation.

Language and terminology

Problems are introduced by language itself: not only is it difficult to verbalise what we see, but in doing so we ossify images which in reality change over time. The language of landscape appreciation, once richly expressive, has lost its interest over the past two centuries and has become degenerate, cliché-ridden and poverty stricken. The social history of landscape terms shows that their use has also changed since the 18th century: 'landscape' was then a key term for understanding the world, including the economic power derived from the use of our environment and its resources. A 'prospect' was a view over an estate, not merely a view in the abstract. Our landscape vocabulary today no longer conveys these resonances, but is impoverished. The words we use do not adequately convey a sense of place, the smells, noises, movement of clouds and the 'feel' of landscape. It cannot convey what impressions remain when one has left a place and which are immediately recognisable on return. We cannot but conclude that landscape language is inadequate, but we must therefore also see it as a controversial area; we should not 'legislate' it into standardisation. The exception to all this is perhaps the language of poetry, which may be capable of recording one individual's reaction to a place; but of course this is an individual reaction, and perhaps not useful for scientific purposes.

The language of intuition and emotion is avoided because we are embarrassed to talk of landscape in these terms or we cannot describe its features or totality as we would wish; more difficult still is describing the interactions between the landscapes and the person. Our educational system de-emotionalises language. Landscape architects suffer from the lack of a public vocabulary and image about landscapes (often 'land' or 'countryside' are used as substitutes). 'Landscape' is thus a term rarely used – only as in, for example, 'the Devon landscape' – and instead we talk merely of 'countryside', or landscape components such as woods, hills and villages.

We are inhibited in using affective language perhaps partly because it is seen as vague and nebulous: incapable of rigorous testing. Terms of emotion and affection are unsuitable in public inquiries because either the adequate words do not exist or they are misunderstood by the public. People are trained to talk technically rather than emotionally. Nevertheless artists have developed a self-expressing language from Ruskin's advocacy of landscape drawing and thereby a developed knowledge of shape; thus language perhaps comes *from* study rather than being a precursor *to* it?

Education and the media

Formal education has created a 'neutral' language of description rather than persuasion: a supposedly objective process of enhancing cognition rather than affection. However, instilling a love for native landscapes could represent mere jingoism while the teaching of detailed understanding could inform only about landscape components rather than a totality: a tree as a tree rather than a frame; a hill as a geological feature rather than an exciting climb. Environmental studies too quickly focus on the minutiae rather than the whole.

More people should be helped to see – even art students take time to appreciate the subtleties of light and shade. Children from city schools are less aware and knowledgeable about landscape than those from country schools who, however, may take it more for granted. Learning to look can be enhanced by learning to draw; photography is no short cut.

Media descriptions of landscapes tend to be superficial and to stress alarming 'facts' and distortions rather than feelings and emotions. Only the best media presentations have any rich or complex sensual quality; landscape needs a David Bellamy (or another Hoskins or Betjeman) to kindle more spirit into public presentations. Education and the media should massage landscapes back into life, by providing a far richer diet than the current fare, although the complexity of landscape emotions and issues seems to hinder mass interest.

Practice and power

A major theme developed by Hal Moggridge is the relationship between two groups of 'actors' in the landscape scene. On the one hand there are the academics, theoreticians, and others engaged in landscape research. On the other there are those professionals in landscape-related practices and those working in government departments or pressure groups active in making decisions within the landscape field. Some spend most of their time thinking and writing about landscape; others, who have too little time for thought, act. The issues here include how to facilitate a better exchange of information between these two 'camps'. What is the worth of 'academic' research to the hard-pressed practitioner, and what is the relevance of practitioners' day-to-day problems and insights to the advancement of fundamental landscape under-standing? We should not underestimate in this context the practitioner's dislike of the academic's apparently over-indulgent view, nor the academic's distrust of the practitioner's short time horizon. Academics have no easy answers (indeed few answers at all!). Specialists are themselves hard-pressed. Practitioners may be forced to work to shorter time horizons than researchers and often want 'cheap and cheerful' products rather than carefully investigated or theoretically sound schemes (whatever they are).

The relation between research and practice is linked with the power that practitioners have to change landscapes, and the sources of this power: from their clients, from government tax incentives, from politicians and from land agents and the many others active in changing what we see. The link arises from an implicit view that the practitioner is constrained from taking a 'broader' view – a more research-orientated, 'academic' and fundamental perspective – by the power of the client. The key to progress thus lies through greater understanding and influence over those with this power.

The question for practitioners viewing the results of academic research is 'how much is it capable of being translated into "action"?' Practitioner and theoretician exchange information but the interface between theory and practice remains unclear. The different professional groups (or interest groups) all need highly detailed information and specific theories but the links with the various researchers and their findings are again tenuous.

Some practitioners, none the less, envisage a greater role for specialists with historical, geological or nature conservation skills and insights, to enable the 'generalist' landscape architect to draw on a wider body of expert knowledge, although a surfeit of specialists could interfere with that all-important 'bond' between the landscape architect and client, especially at the start of a project. Perhaps 'middlemen' are needed to provide practitioners with access to these specialists, and vice versa – a 'supermarket' of landscape skills, or a 'cookery book' manual or directory of people with specialist knowledge. Few practitioners have the time themselves to analyse the theoretical basis or bases of their work, and much existing landscape research is not available in a form they can use.

Academics, practitioners and most others nevertheless all concur in their interest in power. The practitioners, landscape architects and policy makers enjoy a sense of power over landscape, yet at the same time they experience the power of their clients. We need to ask how those concerned about landscape matters can shift the attitudes of those with power, so as to be allowed more resources, more freedom and thus more influence over practice. To analyse power relations, moreover, is to begin an analysis of all the forces influencing landscape evolution – not just the professional's client. To influence landscape evolution

needs insights into both 'theory' and the realities of what might be termed simplistically 'the politics of landscape change'.

Money changes attitudes fastest, some think. Capital transfer tax exemption for British 'Heritage Landscapes' in inheritance settlements is a major vehicle for promoting a change in land-owners' attitudes. At the same time, it can provide an entrée for specialist advice on how to manage the landscapes designated for such exemption. Economic incentives are more potent than pious exhortation: should we not play, therefore, to the self-interest of those with power?

A more general question remains how should economic and political power be harnessed to achieve 'satisfactory' landscapes? Landscape architects feel they are searching for balances behind the power: the most obviously powerful do not always 'win'. Not all successful schemes slavishly follow the clients' whims; professionals also have to promote the case of the relatively weak against the strong, such as individual clients against government organisations at public inquiries.

Nevertheless most power resides with small groups or elites. These groups make choices which affect the history and future of particular landscapes; often such choices are ill-informed or based on stereotypes or prejudices. 'Heritage Landscapes' might mean very different things to a land agent or a chartered surveyor – reinforcing again the significance of cognition and language – yet both are primarily or even solely motivated by economic con-siderations. Should we thus educate our land agents? How far can researchers hope to influence politicians? Before this attempt at influencing others becomes realistic we need to know much more about how attitudes can be changed and about what causes key shifts in environmental belief.

Power involves people, yet we know little of public attitudes and landscape aspirations: for the landscape architect this leads to enforced guesses and a dependence on intuition. Another view is that we do not seek the public's landscape opinions because their taste is so poor! All seem to agree that we know little of what 'ordinary people' think about landscape. This could lead to those with power misusing their influence to the detriment of some 'common good'. Ordinary people *are* concerned, although mostly on well-embedded issues such as National Parks and Green Belts; other issues are perhaps not understood? This leads some to want to make landscape more political; others, on the agricultural side, would like to see it less so. Whether there is support for Kenneth Craik's 'political analysis' of landscape preferences (Ch. 4, p. 55) is unclear, yet there is an implicit recognition that landscape issues do and perhaps should polarise the populace, and that this polarisation does follow at least in some ways the conventional political divides.

An agenda for landscape research

What research can provide inevitably falls short of what practitioners require. But their aims also differ. The landscape practitioner may want a 'cookery book' of theories, techniques, data, and conclusions; research can only yield more hypotheses or incomplete results and insights. The snail-like pace of the advancement of understanding leaves researchers and practitioner alike both frustrated and impatient.

Some caveats about the results of research need noting. Detailed and rigorous study may make the practitioner's task more rather than less difficult, by exposing greater complications than had hitherto been appreciated. Progress, moreover, usually comes in small increments rather than in giant strides. The critical academic's task is at least partly 'subversive'; their findings are as likely to demolish existing conventional wisdom as to support it. Furthermore, testable hypotheses in this research field are likely to be narrow (far narrower than some of the ideas listed below). The rigorous analysis and testing required in both the 'arts' and the 'sciences' inevitably narrows the focus of serious inquiry.

Moreover, there may be a risk in research into landscape 'taste': if we learn what forms our preferences and prejudices cannot tastes be manipulated for ulterior ends?

Listed below are some of the ideas for future research that developed from this symposium. Some of these topics were produced prior to the discussions at Down Hall and some after. What emerges is the striking diversity of ideas and the difficulty of translating these into 'researchable' topics. Also interesting is their emphasis on the need for a better understanding of people's landscape attitudes, meanings and values. This reflects our ignorance about attitudes held by different cultures, different classes, in different countries and related to differing landscapes.

The ideas listed below, then, could comprise some of the items on a future research agenda. They are prime ingredients in a recipe for broadening our understanding of landscape meanings and values. However, deciding the best mix of these ingredients, and the cooking required, will involve further work in concerted and coherent debate amongst practitioners, theoreticians and lovers of landscape alike.

(a) Collation of existing data, research material and bibliographies

The production of a dictionary of landscape terminology.

Assembling and sorting bibliographic material on landscape research.

A biennial register of landscape research interests.

Systematic identification of historic landscapes, their eligibility for conservation and techniques for their management.

A systematic search for 'archetypal' landscapes (e.g. the Devon landscape; the Fenland landscape).

Assembling specific and detailed data on landscape painting and poetry.

(b) Topics for research: theoretical, and/or the language of landscape

The distinction between the concepts 'landscape' and 'environment'.

Comparative cultural and historical study of the landscape idea and attitudes to nature.

Collaborative research between the arts and sciences on symbolism in landscape.

The relations between the economics and aesthetics of landscape gardening.

Classification of division of landscapes by ridge lines (see Appleton 1975, pp. 19 and 206).

Exploration of the hierarchy of levels at which landscape is experienced (i.e. from innate biological to the political level).

The relationship between landscape and political and economic forces.

An analysis of the differences between taste and preferences and prejudices.

An analysis of the language of landscape.

The meaning of landscape for other cultures.

The language of landscape: exploring its social and historical dimensions and implications for present day thought and practice.

(c) Topics for research: historical/historic landscapes

An investigation of the tradition of creating new landscapes.

The relation between the biological and the historical in landscape meaning.

The meaning and value of historic landscapes, including historic parks and gardens, and how they can be enhanced.

Ways of reconciling modern land uses with historic/aesthetic qualities.

A study of footpaths as cultural symbols: their use, value and relevance as heritage features.

(d)   Topics for research: appreciation/experience studies of people's landscape attitudes and feelings

GENERAL

A long-term census of changing landscape tastes (e.g. every five years).

An analysis of the pre-conditioning factors which influence perception and appreciation of landscape.

Human biological reactions to landscape.

'Personality assessments' of key individuals involved in the landscape profession ('what makes us tick?').

An exploration of personal versus communal taste.

Studies of how people become acquainted with new places (see Ch. 4).

Exploring the relationship between familiarity with landscapes and landscape values/meanings/attitudes.

Analysis of the ways that contact with landscape deepens or distorts sensibility.

The process by which landscape values are formed or transmitted (for a specific locality, e.g. Dartmoor).

Values and meanings of 'everyday' landscapes to local residents.

Related to the interpretation of landscapes, what makes people respond and *act* in the ways they do – agreeably or disagreeably.

Research on the appreciation of designed (as opposed to 'natural' or 'wilderness') landscapes.

In relation to evolutionary 'base' hypotheses (e.g. Orians's savanna thesis), testing the public's landscape preferences either using photographs, questionnaires or simply market land prices to establish which landscapes are valued.

A study of the process whereby landscape is perceived, i.e. how people become acquainted with a new place (e.g. at first by analogy, later by use of local vocabulary to describe features etc.).

A project requiring people to simulate preferred landscapes in some way or another (as in the work of the Transport and Road Research Laboratory).

RELATED TO DIFFERENT POPULATION GROUPS

How do landscape meanings and values differ according to people's different experience?

How young children see and evaluate landscape.

An analysis of the landscape experience of different age groups.

The class biases of interest in landscape ('is landscape middle class?').

The differences in taste between social groups, and does one group learn from another (and is the time lag definable?)

How certain specific groups experience and value landscape (e.g. land agents).

Evaluating methods of influencing the values of the land-based professions (i.e. farmers and land agents).

An enquiry into *who* likes *what* (in terms of national and class differences).

The extent to which there are real differences in attitudes to landscape conservation in different countries (i.e. USA and UK).

RELATED TO SPECIFIC LANDSCAPES AND LANDSCAPE FEATURES

An assessment of people's expectations from highly valued landscapes.

The effects of transient phenomena on landscape appreciation.

The meanings and value of water in the landscape.

The role of diversity of form and character in our appreciation of 'fine' landscapes: is aesthetic diversity derived from ecological diversity?

The influence of debilitated 'problem' landscapes on the lives of people who live and work in them.

An investigation of the appropriate meanings and values to be sought and obtained from the redeveloping inner-city landscapes. How can the lives of high-rise dwellers be improved by meaningful landscape within their surroundings?

Related to Jay Appleton's prospect-refuge thesis, how do people respond when they cannot find prospect and refuge in a landscape; what are the contemporary needs for these?

The way people re-value landscapes coming under threat.

(e) Topics for research: arts and artistic studies

How the different arts elicit responses to landscape. How is the sensual experience of one person 'reduced' to the verbal/audio/visual medium to create a sensual response in someone else?

The extent to which landscapes compare qualitatively with the books, music, paintings and films we choose to remember them by.

How are tastes transmitted from poets/writers/artists to ordinary people?

(f)   Topics for research: design/management/interpretation/ education and training

Investigating methods and techniques for creating meaning and value in designed landscapes through the design process.

Participation by researchers within an active and free-ranging design of landscape modifications (with an international dimension).

An analysis of the extent to which presentations to decision-makers (e.g. to a Planning Committee) influence their decisions.

The role of interpretation as a medium between the landscape and the contemporary observer.

The relationship between environmental education and landscape perception.

Evaluating the different ways of training students in landscape assessment.

An evaluation of the best methods of including an awareness of landscape as a *central* part of training courses in architecture, landscape architecture, planning, farming, forestry and estate management, etc.

Reference

Appleton, J. 1975. *The experience of landscape*. London: Wiley.

Appendix: Workshop participants

Charles Anderson – Visiting Professor of English, University of Cambridge, Cambridge, England

Jay Appleton – Professor of Geography, University of Hull, Hull, England

Chris Baines – Landscape Consultant and Lecturer, City of Birmingham Polytechnic, Birmingham, England

Ian Brotherton – Lecturer in Landscape Architecture, University of Sheffield, Sheffield, England

Susan Clifford – Lecturer in Planning, Bartlett School, University College London, London, England

Ralph O. Cobham – Landscape Consultant, Cobham Resource Consultants Ltd, Wantage, Oxford, England

Denis Cosgrove – Lecturer in Geography, University of Loughborough, Loughborough, England

Kenneth Craik – Professor of Psychology, University of California, Berkeley, Berkeley, USA

Stephen Daniels – Lecturer in Geography, University of Nottingham, Nottingham, England

Martin Fitton – Principal Officer, Countryside Commission, Cheltenham, England

Andrew Gilg – Lecturer in Geography, University of Exeter, Exeter, England

John W. Gittins – Amenity Officer, Welsh Water Authority, Brecon, Wales

David Goode – Ecologist, Greater London Council, London, England

Brian Goodey – Lecturer in Planning and Urban Design, Joint Centre for Urban Design, Oxford Polytechnic, Oxford, England

Jeff Haynes – Forward Planning Officer, Exmoor National Park, England

Peter Howard – Lecturer in Landscape Studies, Exeter College of Arts, Exeter, England

John B. Jackson – Lecturer, Sante Fe, New Mexico, USA

Preben Jakobsen – Landscape Architect, Cheltenham College of Art, Cheltenham, England

Ewart Johns – Artist

Ian C. Laurie – Lecturer and Landscape Consultant, University of Manchester, Manchester, England

Mrs Muriel Laverack – Special Adviser on Heritage Landscapes, Department of the Environment, London, England

Charles A. Lewis – Horticulturalist, Moreton Aboretum, Liste, Illinois, USA

Anthony R. Long – Assistant Secretary, CPRE, London, England

David Lowenthal – Professor of Geography, University College London, London, England

Ms Jo Meredith – Conservation and Management Branch, Countryside Commission, Cheltenham, England

Hal T. Moggridge – Professor of Landscape Architecture and Landscape Consultant, University of Sheffield, Sheffield, England

Gordon H. Orians – Director, Institute for Environmental Studies, University of Washington, Seattle, USA

Edmund C. Penning-Rowsell – Professor of Geography and Planning, Middlesex Polytechnic, Enfield, England

Stephanie Plackett – Lecturer, Cambridgeshire College of Arts and Technology, Cambridge, England

Hugh C. Prince – Reader in Geography, University College London, London, England

Allan R. Ruff – Lecturer in Landscape Planning, University of Manchester, Manchester, England

Chris Stratton – Countryside Officer and Landscape Architect, Suffolk County Council, Ipswich, England

Carys Swanwick – Landscape Consultant, Land Use Consultants Ltd, London, England,

Dick Watson – Professor of English, University of Durham, Durham, England

Contributors

Jay Appleton was born in Leeds, England, and is a graduate of Oxford, Durham and Hull Universities. He is Emeritus Professor of the University of Hull where he held a Chair of Geography until 1985. He has also taught in Australia (New England and ANU) and New Zealand (Canterbury). He is the author of *The experience of landscape* (Wiley 1975) and papers on various aspects of landscape as well as historical geography and transport. His work on landscape has emphasised an interdisciplinary approach, not least within the Landscape Research Group of which he was Chairman (1976–8 and 1981–4).

Kenneth Henry Craik received his AB degree from Brown University (1958) and his PhD from the University of California at Berkeley (1964). He is professor in the Department of Psychology and Director of the Institute of Personality Assessment and Research, University of California at Berkeley. He is co-editor (with E. H. Zube) of *Perceiving environmental quality* (Plenum 1976) and (with G. E. McKechnie) of *Personality and the environment* (Sage 1978), and founding co-editor of the *Journal of Environmental Psychology*. He is past president of the division of Environmental Psychology, International Association of Applied Psychology (IAAP), and of the Division of Population and Environmental Psychology, American Psychological Association (APA).

Brian Goodey was born and raised in Essex, studied geography at Nottingham and at Indiana University, and subsequently taught in North Dakota, Birmingham, and Oxford. He is currently Reader in Environmental Design in the Joint Centre for Urban Design at Oxford Polytechnic, and is associated with the graduate programme in that and related fields at the Federal University of Minas Gerais, Brazil. He has written research and reflective monographs on environmental perception, landscape architecture, and planning, and is presently concerned with extending the techniques of interpretive geography to planning and architectural practice.

John Brinckerhoff Jackson graduated from Harvard in 1932. Following service in the U.S. Army (1940–46), he founded *Landscape*, a journal he edited and published between 1951 and 1968. He was Adjunct Professor at the College of Environmental Design, University of California at Berkeley, from 1967 to 1977, and Visiting Professor, Department of Landscape Architecture, Harvard University, from 1969 to 1977, teaching there also in the Department of Visual and Environmental Studies. Made Honorary Doctor of Fine Arts at the University of New Mexico in 1977, Jackson was Carl Sauer Memorial Lecturer at the University of California, Berkeley, in 1978, and Visiting Professor at the University of Texas in 1980. His books include *Landscapes* (1971), *American space* (1974), *The necessity for ruins* (1980), *Exploring the vernacular landscape* (1984), and *The essential landscape* (1985).

Hal Moggridge was trained at the Architectural Association and as a landscape architect while working under Sir Geoffrey Jellicoe. In 1969 he founded the firm of Colvin and Moggridge with the late Brenda Colvin. The landscapes he has designed throughout the UK include Brenig Reservoir, Torr Quarry, White Horse Hill Car Park, Gale Common Ash Hill, the garden of Jesus College Oxford, and restoration projects for Lancelot ('Capability') Brown's Blenheim Park and Cadland Garden. President of the Landscape Institute from 1979 to 1981, he is currently its representative on the International Federation of Landscape Architects and the Management Advisory Board for the Glasgow Garden Festival, 1988.

Gordon H. Orians is Professor of Zoology and Director of the Institute for Environmental Studies at the University of Washington, Seattle. His research fields include behavioural ecology, especially such aspects as habitat selection, foraging theory, and social organization, plant–herbivore interactions, and the preservation of biological resources. His interest in landscape aesthetics grew out of his studies of habitat selection processes among birds and reflects his general orientation towards applying evolutionary thinking to a wide variety of issues and problems. He is author of several books and over fifty scientific articles.

Index

Museums of Rural Life 85
music and the sense of place 41

Nairn, I. 85, 95
National Heritage Act 1983 110
National Trust
    United Kingdom 88, 99, 118
    United States of America 56, 58
natural selection, influence of 6, 10,
    17–18, 23, 25
Nicholson, Norman 27–8, 31–2, 43
Norton-Griffiths, M. 10
le Nôtre, André 38, 39, 107

open field system 72, 74
    decay of 76
Ordnance Survey maps 79
Orians, G. H. 3–25, 117, 126

'pagus' 65
painting, painters 16, 30–1, 45–6
    prints and reproductions 88–9
    'serial vision' 41
    socialist realism 87
    subject/technique 39
    urban subjects 87
    way of 'reading' a landscape 41, 82
parks
    National Parks 87, 109, 123
    see also gardens
Partridge, L. 3
pattern perception 25, 49
    'stimulus discrepancy' 19
Paulson, R. 42
Pavlov, I. P. 19
Penning-Rowsell, E. C. viii–ix,
    114–28
photographs of landscapes 15–16, 35,
    87
    as aid to landscape evaluation 48
    Bill Brandt 87
Pianka, E. R. 3
Pidgley, M. 36
'place, the sense of' 63, 120
plants, plant shapes 3, 17, 102
poetry, the poetic imagination 27–8,
    31–2, 35, 41, 43, 77, 120
Pope, Alexander 40
Priestley, J. B. 89
Prince, H. 35, 41
profit-motive, its effect on landscape
    112–13, 116, 122–3
psychology, environmental 48–64, 35
    cognitive categories 52

environmental inferences 53
landscape cognition/meaning 51–3
landscape perception through the
    minds of others 51, 55
rôle enactment 50
symbolism 39, 40, 53

recreation see landscape, public
    amenity
Reid, Thomas 17, 20
Repton, H. 111
research, suggestions for 124–8, ix, 2,
    8, 34, 45, 55
    academic vs. 'practical' subjects
    121–3
    aesthetics 111
    education 96–7, 120–1
    problems of practice 109–12
    topics related to environmental psy-
    chology 56–9
Robinson, J. I. 10
Romantic movement 36, 80, 106
Rosch, E. 52, 57
Rosenzweig, M. L. 3
Rowe, R. D. 58
Royal Institution (London), meeting at
    viii, ix
rural pursuits (e.g. fishing, hunting)
    94, 101
Ruskin, John 120
Russell, J. A. 52

Santayana, G. 18
savanna regions 10–15, 16, 23, 24, 117
Save Britain's Heritage 56
'scape', etymology of 67
    use today 84–5
Shelley, Percy Bysshe 24, 46
Sibelius, J. 42
Sinclair, A. R. E. 10
Slovic, P. 53
Smardon, R. C. 58
Sontag, Susan 86
Stark, Freya 63
structuralist theory 23
students, landscape studies with 50, 80,
    83–4, 96–7
symbolism 39–40
    symbolic meanings of landscape
    115

taste, aesthetic 34, 37–8, 40, 52, 84–5,
    119, 123–4
    'English Landscape Taste' 84–5, 88,